MANAGEMENT AND LEADERSHIP PRINCIPLES OF JESUS

Based on the Book of Mark

Temitope Ajagbe

My Fathers House Teaching Ministries

ISBN-13: 9798300220556
ISBN-10: 1477123456

Cover design by: Art Painter
Library of Congress Control Number: 2018675309
Printed in the United States of America

CONTENTS

INTRODUCTION

Leadership is one of the most profound and challenging responsibilities we can undertake. Whether leading an organization, a team, a community, or a family, the role of a leader requires vision, resilience, integrity, and the ability to inspire and guide others. In a world often driven by metrics, power, and influence, the question arises: Is there a model of leadership that prioritizes purpose, service, and enduring impact?

The answer can be found in the life and teachings of Jesus, as recorded in the Gospel of Mark. In just 16 chapters, Mark presents Jesus as a dynamic and transformative leader, navigating complex socio-political challenges, empowering a diverse group of followers, and maintaining unwavering focus on His mission. His leadership was revolutionary, rooted not in self-promotion but in humility, compassion, and a commitment to serving others.

This book, *Management and Leadership Principles of Jesus*, explores how the timeless principles Jesus modeled can inspire and equip modern leaders across industries and contexts. From casting a clear vision to handling opposition, redefining success, and building a legacy, these principles are not bound by time or culture. They offer guidance for navigating the challenges of leadership while remaining grounded in purpose and integrity.

In each chapter, we will examine a leadership principle demonstrated by Jesus, drawing insights from the Gospel of Mark. We will then apply these principles to contemporary leadership scenarios, exploring how they can be implemented in fields as diverse as healthcare, government, business, and education. The inclusion of real-world examples and practical strategies ensures that these lessons are accessible and actionable for leaders at all levels.

Whether you are leading a team, an organization, or simply yourself, this book invites you to reflect on your approach to leadership. It challenges you to embrace a model of leadership that prioritizes service over status, impact over accolades, and purpose over profit. In doing so, you will not only transform how you lead but also inspire others to join you in creating meaningful, lasting change.

Leadership is not just about what we achieve but about the lives we touch and the legacy we leave behind. Let us embark on this journey together, learning from the greatest leader in history and discovering how to lead with purpose, faith, and courage.

INTRODUCTION

When we think of the greatest leaders in history, certain names might come to mind—visionaries who inspired movements, shaped nations, or revolutionized industries. Yet, one name stands apart from them all: Jesus of Nazareth (the Christ). More than two thousand years ago, He walked the earth, not as a monarch or military commander, but as a humble teacher, healer, and servant and savior. Through His life, as recorded in the Gospel of Mark, we find an extraordinary model of leadership and management—one that transcends time, culture, and industry.

The Gospel of Mark is the shortest and most action-packed of the four gospels, giving us a fast-paced narrative of Jesus' ministry. It presents a leader who is decisive yet compassionate, bold yet humble, and authoritative yet approachable. Jesus led with a clear mission, empowered a small and diverse team to carry out a global vision, and transformed lives through His innovative and adaptable methods. His leadership principles, though rooted in first-century Judea, are profoundly relevant for today's leaders navigating complex challenges in the 21st century.

This book explores Jesus' leadership through the lens of the Gospel of Mark, a treasure trove of lessons for anyone seeking to lead with purpose, integrity, and lasting impact. We will see how Jesus cast a compelling vision, prioritized time for what mattered most, communicated with clarity and wisdom, and handled opposition with grace. We will also witness how He empowered others, managed crises, and ultimately prepared His followers to carry on His mission after His departure.

Jesus' leadership style defies convention. While many leaders strive to assert control, He embraced servant leadership. While others built empires, He built people. His approach wasn't about climbing to the top but about lifting others. This radical approach not only changed the world but continues to inspire leaders today, from CEOs and managers to teachers, parents, and community organizers.

Why focus exclusively on the Gospel of Mark? Because its vivid and concise narrative reveals Jesus in action—a leader constantly on the move, making decisions, confronting challenges, and teaching through example. Mark's gospel is not just a record of what Jesus did but a guide to how He led. By immersing ourselves in its pages, we gain not only a deeper understanding of Jesus' leadership but also practical insights to transform our own.

This book is not about theological debates or religious doctrines; rather, it is a practical exploration of timeless principles that anyone—regardless of faith—can apply in their leadership journey. Whether you are leading a business, a family, a nonprofit, or a team of any kind, the lessons from Jesus' life will inspire and equip you to lead with greater confidence, compassion, and effectiveness.

Join me as we embark on this journey through the Gospel of Mark, uncovering the management and leadership principles of Jesus. Together, we will discover how His example can transform not only how we lead but also how we live.

CHAPTER 1: VISION AND MISSION

◆ ◆ ◆

From the opening verses of the Gospel of Mark, Jesus bursts onto the scene with a sense of urgency and clarity. He announces, "The time has come... The kingdom of God has come near. Repent and believe the good news!" (Mark 1:15, NIV). This proclamation sets the tone for His ministry, revealing a vision that is both revolutionary and deeply countercultural. Unlike leaders who test the waters before launching their mission, Jesus begins decisively, demonstrating a confidence rooted in divine purpose.

The Scope of Jesus' Growth Plan

At first glance, Jesus' strategy seems paradoxical. His vision is immense: to proclaim the Kingdom of God to all humanity. Yet, He begins in the obscure region of Galilee, focusing on individuals and small gatherings rather than massive crowds or political structures. This deliberate choice reflects a leadership philosophy that prioritizes depth over breadth.

Jesus' initial recruits—fishermen like Peter, Andrew, James, and John—are ordinary individuals with no formal theological training or societal influence (Mark 1:16-20). This stands in stark contrast to the prevailing expectation that a revolutionary leader would seek alliances with the elite or powerful. Jesus' approach suggests a belief that genuine transformation begins with personal relationships and the cultivation of committed individuals who can carry the mission forward.

The tension here is clear: how can such a grand vision be realized with such modest beginnings? Jesus' approach challenges the notion that effective leadership requires immediate large-scale impact. Instead, He demonstrates that a well-prepared foundation, even if small, can sustain and multiply growth over time.

Opposition to the Vision

From the outset, Jesus faces resistance, much of it rooted in entrenched religious and cultural norms. His proclamation of the Kingdom is seen as a threat to both the Roman authorities and the Jewish religious leaders. For the Romans, the idea of a "kingdom" other than Caesar's was politically subversive. For the religious leaders, Jesus' emphasis on repentance and direct access to God undermined their control and the legalistic systems they upheld.

For instance, in Mark 2:6-12, Jesus forgives a paralyzed man's sins, prompting the religious leaders to accuse Him of blasphemy. This moment reveals a key tension: Jesus' mission is not about maintaining or reforming existing power structures but about introducing an entirely new paradigm. His focus on internal transformation—repentance, faith, and personal relationship with God—challenged the prevailing thought that righteousness could be achieved solely through external adherence to the law.

Despite this opposition, Jesus remains unwavering. His response to critics is often characterized by calm authority and an ability to reframe the discussion. Rather than being swayed by resistance, He uses these moments to clarify His vision and further distinguish His mission from societal expectations.

Philosophical Tensions in Jesus' Approach

One of the most profound philosophical tensions in Jesus' leadership is His rejection of traditional metrics of success. In a society dominated by hierarchy, status, and visible power, Jesus measures success by faithfulness to the mission and the transformation of hearts. This is most evident in His parables, such as the Parable of the Sower (Mark 4:1-20), where He emphasizes the importance of fertile soil—prepared hearts— over superficial appearances of growth.

Additionally, Jesus embodies a paradoxical balance of urgency and patience. While He repeatedly emphasizes that "the time has come," He also allows time for His disciples to learn, fail, and grow. For example, His decision to teach in parables (Mark 4:10-12) reflects His understanding of the need for gradual revelation. He avoids forcing His vision on those unready to receive it, demonstrating a deep respect for the process of personal growth and understanding.

Influence of the Prevailing Thought Process

The prevailing religious and cultural thought of the time was steeped in legalism, tradition, and a transactional view of God. Many leaders of Jesus' era believed in enforcing adherence to the law as the primary means of maintaining societal order and religious purity. Jesus disrupts this mindset by focusing on the spirit rather than the letter of the law. For example, when questioned about His disciples picking grain on the Sabbath, He declares, "The Sabbath was made for man, not man for the Sabbath" (Mark 2:27). This statement reflects His larger philosophy: rules and systems exist to serve people, not the other way around.

Interestingly, while the prevailing thought often opposed Jesus, it also shaped His approach in some ways. Jesus frequently engages with the cultural and religious framework of His audience, using it as a starting point to introduce new ideas. His use of Scripture in debates with religious leaders (e.g., Mark 12:10-11) demonstrates a willingness to meet people where they are, even as He challenges them to think differently.

Lessons for Modern Leaders

For leaders today, Jesus' vision and mission offer several key lessons:

1. **Start Small, Think Big**: Effective leaders don't need to have all the resources or influence upfront. What matters is clarity of vision and commitment to building a strong foundation.
2. **Stay True Despite Opposition**: Resistance is inevitable, but leaders who remain focused on their purpose can turn opposition into opportunities for growth and clarity.
3. **Balance Urgency with Patience**: Leaders must know when to act decisively and when to allow time for growth and understanding.
4. **Challenge the Status Quo Thoughtfully**: Disruption is most effective when it is grounded in respect for people and a clear articulation of why change is necessary.

As we continue to explore Jesus' leadership in the Gospel of Mark, we see that His vision for the Kingdom of God is not just a lofty ideal but a practical framework for leading with purpose, compassion, and resilience.

Case Study: Healthcare Technology Startup

The Vision: Empowering Global Health Independence

Imagine a healthcare technology startup, Health Empower, with a bold mission: to revolutionize how global consumers prevent, manage, and maintain their health. The platform offers tools for individuals to track their health metrics, manage medical records, and gain actionable insights—all while bypassing traditional healthcare power brokers like employer insurance subsidies, government plans, and large healthcare systems.

Health Empower envisions a world where individuals are in full control of their health decisions, guided by a seamless and intuitive platform that prioritizes privacy, accessibility, and affordability. However, the company faces significant challenges, including competition from established healthcare systems, skepticism from consumers, and regulatory barriers.

By applying the leadership principles modeled by Jesus in the Gospel of Mark, Health Empower can address these challenges and establish a strong foundation for sustainable growth.

1. Start Small, Think Big

Jesus' Principle: Begin with a clear vision and invest deeply in a small group.

In Mark 1:16-20, Jesus calls His first disciples—fishermen who had no influence or specialized training. This small, committed team became the foundation of a movement that transformed the world.

Application

Health Empower should begin by identifying a focused target audience. Instead of trying to appeal to everyone globally, the startup could initially focus on a specific demographic, such as young professionals in urban areas who lack employer-sponsored insurance. By solving the pain points of this niche audience and deeply understanding their needs, the company can create a loyal user base that acts as advocates for the platform.

Additionally, the leadership team should be handpicked, emphasizing alignment with the mission over mere technical qualifications. This ensures that everyone involved shares a passion for the vision.

2. Serve the Needs of the Users

**Jesus' Principle: Lead by serving others
and addressing their real needs.**

Mark 10:42-45 reveals Jesus' philosophy of servant leadership, emphasizing that greatness comes from serving others.

Application

Health Empower's platform must be designed with the user's needs at its core. Instead of replicating existing systems, it should offer features that empower users with autonomy and insight, such as:

- **Customizable Health Dashboards**: Tailored to individual health goals.

- **Affordable Subscription Plans**: Offering premium tools without hidden costs.
- **Privacy-First Approach**: Ensuring users maintain full ownership of their data.

By prioritizing the user experience and solving tangible problems, Health Empower demonstrates its commitment to serving its customers rather than profiting from their dependence on complex systems.

3. Navigate Opposition with Clarity and Confidence

Jesus' Principle: Face opposition with calm authority, focusing on the mission.

In Mark 2:6-12, Jesus forgives sins and heals a paralyzed man, provoking outrage from religious leaders. Instead of avoiding conflict, He uses it to clarify His mission and challenge the status quo.

Application
Health Empower will likely face opposition from entrenched power brokers, such as large insurance companies and healthcare systems. To navigate this, the company should:

- **Communicate the Mission Clearly**: Develop a narrative that explains how the platform empowers users without attacking existing systems.
- **Anticipate and Address Concerns**: Prepare thoughtful responses to criticisms about affordability, accessibility, and reliability.
- **Focus on Impact**: Highlight success stories from early users to build credibility and counter opposition with evidence of real-world benefits.

4. Innovate and Challenge the Status Quo

Jesus' Principle: Introduce a new paradigm while respecting tradition.

In Mark 2:18-22, Jesus introduces the idea that new wine requires new wineskins, signaling the need for innovation while respecting what is valuable in the old system.

Application

Health Empower must embrace innovation while addressing users' attachment to traditional healthcare systems. For instance:

- **Leverage AI and Machine Learning**: Offer predictive analytics for early detection of health issues.
- **Introduce New Payment Models**: Allow users to pay based on outcomes or value derived, instead of flat fees.
- **Provide Transparent Access**: Develop partnerships with independent healthcare providers to offer discounted consultations outside the insurance framework.

By showing respect for existing systems (e.g., offering data integration with hospital records) while demonstrating the advantages of their model, Health Empower can create a compelling alternative.

5. Build a Scalable Foundation

Jesus' Principle: Prepare a team for multiplication and growth.

In Mark 6:7-13, Jesus sends His disciples out in pairs, empowering them to carry His mission forward independently. This decentralized model ensured scalability.

Application

Health Empower should design its platform for scalability from the beginning:

- **Global-Friendly Architecture**: Build a robust cloud-based infrastructure that can scale to handle diverse users across regions.
- **Training and Education**: Empower local healthcare providers, tech support teams, and user advocates to represent the platform globally.
- **Community Building**: Encourage users to share insights and create local support networks, turning them into ambassadors of the platform.

6. Measure Success Differently

Jesus' Principle: Redefine success as transformation, not just metrics.

In Mark 4:1-20, the Parable of the Sower highlights that success lies not in the number of seeds scattered but in the depth of the fruit they bear.

Application
Health Empower should measure its success by the outcomes it enables for its users, not just the number of sign-ups or app downloads. Metrics might include:

- Improvement in users' health metrics (e.g., reduced HbA1c for diabetics).
- Increased user confidence in managing their own health.
- Positive feedback on user experience and trustworthiness of the platform.

7. Prepare for Long-Term Impact

Jesus' Principle: Focus on legacy and multiplication.

In Mark 16:15-20, Jesus commissions His disciples to continue

His work, ensuring the mission's continuation after His departure.

Application

Health Empower should establish structures for long-term sustainability:

- **Partnering with Educational Institutions**: Train the next generation of healthcare innovators.
- **Investing in Research**: Use data insights to improve global health strategies.
- **Planning for Leadership Succession**: Develop a robust leadership pipeline to ensure the company's mission survives beyond its founders.

Conclusion

By applying the leadership principles modeled by Jesus, Health Empower can overcome challenges, foster trust, and create a sustainable impact. Jesus' example reminds us that successful leadership is not about dominating the market or conforming to societal expectations but about serving others, staying true to a clear vision, and building a foundation that transforms lives over time. Just as Jesus' small team of disciples catalyzed a global movement, Health Empower can create a healthcare revolution, one empowered individual at a time.

CHAPTER 2:
RECRUITING AND
EMPOWERING
A TEAM

◆ ◆ ◆

In the Gospel of Mark, one of the first significant actions Jesus takes is assembling His team of disciples. This is no small task. The success of His mission depended on individuals who would not only follow Him but also carry His vision forward after His earthly ministry ended. His choices, methods, and interactions with His team provide a masterclass in recruiting and empowering people for a transformative mission.

For leaders and managers today, particularly in dynamic industries like technology and healthcare, building and empowering a team is often the most critical and challenging aspect of leadership. This chapter delves into Jesus' approach, highlighting the underlying principles and practical applications for modern leaders.

The Call To Discipleship: Building With Purpose

In Mark 1:16-20, Jesus calls Simon (Peter), Andrew, James, and John to leave their fishing nets and follow Him. These men are not scholars, politicians, or religious elites—they are ordinary laborers. Yet Jesus sees their potential and invites them into a mission far greater than their current reality: "Follow me, and I will make you fishers of men" (Mark 1:17, NIV).

1. Jesus' Selection Criteria

- **Potential Over Credentials**: Jesus doesn't choose based on societal status, education, or expertise. Instead, He looks for qualities like teachability, commitment, and willingness to embrace change.
- **Alignment with the Vision**: His call emphasizes the mission from the outset, making it clear that following Him involves both transformation and purpose.

Modern Application

In a startup environment, particularly one in healthcare technology like *Health Empower*, leaders often face the temptation to prioritize resumes over values. Jesus' example suggests that hiring for character, adaptability, and alignment with the company's mission may be more critical for long-term success than technical expertise alone. The ideal team member is someone who can grow with the organization, not just fill an immediate skill gap.

The Invitation To Belong

Jesus' approach to recruitment is not transactional. He doesn't merely assign tasks or offer incentives. Instead, He invites His disciples into a relationship and a community. This sense of belonging is central to His leadership philosophy.

2. Building Trust Through Relationships

- **Personal Engagement**: Jesus calls His disciples individually, speaking directly to their hearts and lives.
- **Creating a Shared Purpose**: By casting a vision that resonates personally—becoming "fishers of men"—Jesus ties their individual identities to a larger mission.

Modern Application

In leading a healthcare technology startup, fostering a sense of belonging is essential, especially in a fast-paced, high-stakes environment. Leaders should:

- Take time to know team members personally, understanding their motivations and goals.
- Create a culture of shared purpose where every role is clearly connected to the company's mission of empowering global health independence.

Empowerment Through Delegation

In Mark 6:7-13, Jesus sends His disciples out two by two, giving them authority to preach, heal, and cast out demons. This delegation is remarkable because it occurs early in their journey, before they have mastered the complexities of Jesus' teachings.

3. Trusting People to Succeed (and Fail)

- **Authority Without Micromanagement**: Jesus entrusts His disciples with real responsibility, empowering them to act on His behalf.

- **Learning Through Experience**: By sending them out, Jesus allows them to learn firsthand, even if it means making mistakes.

Modern Application

For a startup like *Health Empower*, empowering team members with autonomy can accelerate innovation and growth. Leaders can:

- Delegate meaningful responsibilities early, even if employees are still learning.
- Provide a safe environment for experimentation and learning from failure.

This principle also applies to empowering users. For instance, *Health Empower* could encourage early adopters to shape the platform through feedback, making them co-creators in its development.

Cultivating A Growth Mindset

Jesus repeatedly challenges His disciples to grow, even when they struggle to understand or keep up. In Mark 4:40, after calming a storm, He asks, "Why are you so afraid? Do you still have no faith?" Such moments, though uncomfortable, push the disciples to develop deeper trust and resilience.

4. Balancing Support and Challenge

- **Encouragement in Weakness**: Jesus never abandons His disciples when they falter, but He also doesn't shy away from pointing out their shortcomings.
- **Providing Opportunities for Growth**: Each challenge is a step toward greater maturity and preparedness for the

mission.

Modern Application

In the context of *Health Empower*, leaders can foster growth by:

- Providing regular feedback that is both constructive and affirming.
- Setting ambitious but achievable goals, encouraging team members to stretch their capabilities.

For example, a junior developer might be entrusted with leading a critical feature rollout, with mentorship provided along the way. This approach cultivates confidence and competence simultaneously.

Diversity And Unity In The Team

Mark 3:13-19 lists the twelve apostles, a group that includes fishermen, a tax collector (Matthew), a zealot (Simon), and Judas Iscariot, who would later betray Jesus. This diverse group brings different skills, perspectives, and even conflicting ideologies to the table.

5. Embracing Diversity for Strength

- **Unified by Purpose**: Despite their differences, the disciples are united by their shared commitment to Jesus' vision.
- **Leveraging Individual Strengths**: Each disciple contributes uniquely to the mission, whether it's Peter's boldness or John's depth of understanding.

Modern Application

Startups thrive on diversity of thought and experience. Leaders at *Health Empower* should:

- Assemble teams with varied professional backgrounds, such as technology, healthcare, and user advocacy.
- Foster a culture where diverse perspectives are valued and conflicts are resolved through open communication and a shared commitment to the mission.

Sustaining The Team Through Challenges

As Jesus' ministry grows, the demands on the disciples increase, and their shortcomings become evident. Yet Jesus continues to mentor and guide them, preparing them for the time when they will carry the mission forward without Him.

6. Preparing for Longevity

- **Continuous Training**: Jesus consistently teaches through parables, discussions, and demonstrations, ensuring His disciples are equipped for the future.
- **Modeling Resilience**: Through His own actions, Jesus shows how to navigate rejection, opposition, and hardship.

Modern Application

In a startup environment, burnout and turnover are common risks. Leaders can sustain their teams by:

- Investing in ongoing professional development, such as workshops on emerging healthcare trends or leadership training.
- Modeling work-life balance and resilience, ensuring the team stays motivated through inevitable challenges.

A Team That Transforms The World

Jesus' approach to building and empowering His team was

revolutionary. By focusing on potential, fostering relationships, delegating authority, and embracing diversity, He created a team capable of sustaining and expanding His mission.

For *Health Empower*, the lessons are clear: success doesn't come from hiring the most polished resumes or micromanaging every detail. Instead, it's about cultivating a team that believes in the mission, grows through challenges, and works together to create lasting impact. Just as Jesus' small band of disciples transformed the world, a well-built and empowered team can revolutionize healthcare, one empowered individual at a time.

Identifying Potential: Seeing Beyond the Surface

◆ ◆ ◆

I n Mark 1:16-20, Jesus calls His first disciples—ordinary fishermen—inviting them to leave their nets and follow Him. On the surface, these men lacked the credentials to be part of a world-changing mission. They were not scholars, religious leaders, or influencers of their day. Yet, Jesus saw potential in them that others may have overlooked.

1. Look for Character, Not Just Skills

Jesus chose disciples not for their current skills but for their teachable spirits, commitment, and willingness to grow.

- **Peter**: Impulsive and flawed, yet bold and loyal.
- **James and John**: Ambitious, yet deeply devoted to Jesus' mission.

Modern Application:
For a leader in a healthcare technology startup like *Health Empower*, identifying potential means looking beyond resumes and technical skills to discern deeper qualities such as:

- **Adaptability**: Can this person learn quickly and thrive in a fast-changing environment?
- **Passion for the Mission**: Are they genuinely motivated by the company's vision to empower individuals in healthcare?
- **Collaborative Spirit**: Can they work well with others, especially in a diverse and interdisciplinary team?

Practical Tips for Leaders

- Conduct behavioral interviews to assess how candidates handle challenges and learn from failures.
- Use situational tasks to observe problem-solving abilities and team dynamics in action.
- Look for alignment with organizational values and mission during interviews.

2. Spotting Hidden Talent

Jesus often saw potential in individuals that others missed. For example, in Mark 2:13-17, He calls Levi (Matthew), a tax collector—a profession despised in Jewish society. Levi's social position and occupation made him an unlikely candidate, yet Jesus saw his ability to connect with outcasts and later write one of the Gospels.

Modern Application
Leaders should adopt an inclusive mindset, considering

unconventional candidates who might bring fresh perspectives. For example:

- A user advocate with no formal healthcare background might excel in identifying real-world pain points.
- A data analyst from a nontraditional career path might bring innovative methods for predictive health modeling.

The Tension in Incentives: What Motivates People to Join a Mission?

Recruiting the right people often involves balancing two forces: the clarity of the mission and the tension surrounding incentives. Jesus' call to discipleship, as recorded in Mark, is notable for its lack of conventional incentives. He offers no financial rewards, no promises of power, and no clear personal benefits. Instead, His recruitment pitch focuses on purpose and transformation: "Follow me, and I will make you fishers of men" (Mark 1:17, NIV).

This approach raises critical questions for modern leaders:

- What drives people to join a mission when traditional incentives are absent or insufficient?
- How can leaders navigate the tension between intrinsic motivations (purpose, impact) and extrinsic rewards (salary, perks)?

1. Jesus' Approach: Purpose Over Perks

Jesus' recruitment strategy relies entirely on the power of His vision. He invites the disciples into a mission that is larger than themselves—one that promises significance and eternal impact. His statement, "fishers of men," reframes their existing identity and skills (as fishermen) into a higher calling.

The Tension of Sacrifice

Jesus does not shy away from the cost of discipleship. Later in Mark, He tells His followers, "Whoever wants to be my disciple must deny themselves and take up their cross and follow me" (Mark 8:34). This stark warning highlights the sacrificial nature of the mission, creating a tension between the promise of significance and the reality of personal cost.

The Clarity of the Vision

Despite the sacrifices, Jesus' clarity about the mission inspires commitment. He articulates the goal—a new Kingdom of God—and models the values that define this Kingdom: humility, service, and love. This clarity resonates deeply with His disciples, giving them a sense of direction and purpose that outweighs the absence of traditional incentives.

Modern Application:

For a healthcare technology startup like *Health Empower*, where traditional incentives (e.g., high salaries, stability) may be limited, leaders can follow Jesus' example by emphasizing:

- **Purpose**: Frame the work as a chance to transform global healthcare and empower individuals to take control of their health.
- **Personal Growth**: Highlight opportunities for learning, innovation, and professional development.
- **Community Impact**: Show how the team's efforts directly benefit underserved populations, giving employees a sense of pride and connection to the mission.

2. Navigating The Tension Between Intrinsic And Extrinsic Incentives

While Jesus prioritized intrinsic motivation, modern organizations must often balance this with practical extrinsic rewards to attract and retain talent. The tension arises when extrinsic incentives risk overshadowing or diluting the mission.

Intrinsic Motivation: The Power of Purpose

Jesus relied heavily on intrinsic motivation, which is driven by:

- **Meaningful Work**: The disciples understood that their efforts had eternal significance.
- **Identity Transformation**: They were called not just to work but to become something greater ("fishers of men").
- **Belonging**: Joining Jesus' mission meant becoming part of a close-knit, purpose-driven community.

Modern Application:
Startups can tap into intrinsic motivation by:

- Clearly communicating the impact of the work (e.g., how the technology helps individuals manage chronic illnesses or access care).
- Offering roles that align with employees' personal values and aspirations.
- Creating a strong team culture where individuals feel valued and connected.

Extrinsic Rewards: Balancing Practical Needs

While intrinsic motivation is powerful, practical needs cannot be ignored. Jesus, for example, provided for His disciples' basic needs (e.g., food, lodging), ensuring they could focus on the mission.

Modern Application

Leaders must offer competitive, though not necessarily extravagant, extrinsic rewards:

- **Fair Compensation**: While startups may not match corporate salaries, they can offer equity, bonuses tied to mission milestones, or creative perks.
- **Flexibility**: Allow team members to balance their personal and professional lives through flexible schedules or remote work.
- **Recognition**: Publicly celebrate achievements to show that contributions are valued.

Avoiding Dependency on Extrinsic Incentives

Excessive reliance on extrinsic rewards can undermine intrinsic motivation. Studies in behavioral psychology show that when financial rewards are the primary focus, employees may lose sight of the mission.

Leaders can navigate this tension by:

- Framing extrinsic rewards as a means to support the mission, not the end goal.
- Linking rewards to outcomes that align with the company's vision (e.g., bonuses for innovations that improve patient outcomes).

3. Transparency About Challenges And Rewards

Jesus was remarkably transparent about the challenges His disciples would face. In Mark 13:9-13, He warns them of persecution and hardship, yet He also assures them of the ultimate reward: being part of God's Kingdom. This honesty builds trust and ensures that the disciples are fully committed, even when the path becomes difficult.

Modern Application

Transparency is essential for recruiting and retaining talent in a startup environment. Leaders should:

- Be upfront about the challenges of working in a startup, such as long hours, uncertainty, and limited resources.
- Emphasize the unique opportunities that offset these challenges, such as creative freedom, rapid career growth, and the chance to make a tangible impact.
- Regularly communicate both short-term goals and long-term vision, ensuring that employees understand the company's direction and their role within it.

4. Incentives As A Tool For Retention, Not Recruitment

In Mark 6:30-31, after the disciples return from their mission, Jesus says, "Come with me by yourselves to a quiet place and get some rest." This moment illustrates how Jesus cared for His team's well-being, ensuring they were not only motivated but also sustained for the long haul.

Modern Application

While mission-driven startups may rely on purpose to attract talent, they must use incentives strategically to retain it. For example:

- **Wellness Programs**: Offer resources to support mental and physical health, such as gym memberships or meditation apps.
- **Professional Development**: Provide opportunities for employees to grow within the company through mentorship, training, or leadership roles.
- **Recognition of Effort**: Celebrate milestones and acknowledge hard work, even if results are still in progress.

Crafting An Incentive Strategy Rooted In Purpose

Jesus' approach to recruitment demonstrates that the most powerful incentive is a compelling vision of purpose and transformation. By prioritizing intrinsic motivation while addressing practical needs, He built a team that was not only committed to the mission but also resilient in the face of challenges.

For a healthcare technology startup like *Health Empower*, navigating the tension between intrinsic and extrinsic incentives requires clarity, transparency, and intentionality. Leaders must articulate a vision that inspires, provide the support necessary to sustain the team, and ensure that rewards enhance—rather than compete with—the mission. When done well, this balance creates a team that is not only capable but also passionate about driving meaningful change in the world.

The Challenge of Retaining or
Removing a Potential Betrayer

One of the most perplexing aspects of Jesus' leadership in the Gospel of Mark is His decision to include Judas Iscariot, knowing Judas would eventually betray Him. In Mark 3:13-19, Jesus calls Judas alongside the other disciples, granting him the same authority and responsibilities as the rest. Judas preaches, heals, and even represents Jesus' mission. Yet, in Mark 14:10-11, Judas actively conspires with the chief priests to betray Jesus.

This tension raises a critical question for leaders: How do you handle a team member whose loyalty to the mission is questionable? Should you attempt to guide and retain them, or is it better to remove them before they can cause harm? For modern leaders, especially in startups or mission-driven organizations, this dilemma often plays out in the context of team dynamics, organizational culture, and the long-term health of the mission.

1. The Tension Between Inclusion And Risk

Jesus' Decision to Include Judas

Jesus' decision to include Judas reflects a deliberate willingness to invest in someone despite their flaws and potential for betrayal. It highlights a tension between the hope for transformation and the risk of harm to the mission.

- **Belief in Redemption:** Jesus' inclusion of Judas suggests a commitment to offering every individual the opportunity to grow and align with the mission.
- **Strategic Risk Management:** By keeping Judas close, Jesus may have been better able to monitor his actions and

protect the team from external threats.

Modern Application

In a leadership context, this tension often arises when a team member exhibits behaviors that conflict with the organization's values or goals. For example:

- A talented developer may deliver exceptional work but undermine team morale through toxic behavior.
- A business partner might contribute valuable resources while pursuing self-serving goals that conflict with the mission.

Leaders must weigh:

- **The potential for growth or alignment**: Can this person's behavior or attitude be redirected to support the mission?
- **The risk of harm**: How might their continued presence affect the team's cohesion, morale, or long-term goals?

2. Red Flags And Signs Of Betrayal

In Judas' case, several warning signs hint at his eventual betrayal. For example, Judas questions Mary's anointing of Jesus in Mark 14:4-5, framing it as wasteful. His critique suggests a misalignment with Jesus' values, prioritizing material concerns over spiritual devotion.

Key Indicators of Potential Betrayal

Leaders should be alert to behaviors that signal a potential misalignment with the mission, such as:

- **Undermining Team Values**: Openly criticizing decisions or actions that align with the organization's core principles.

- **Self-Serving Actions**: Prioritizing personal gain or recognition over team goals.
- **Erosion of Trust**: Engaging in secretive behavior or withholding critical information.

Modern Example:
In a healthcare technology startup, a team member might:

- Dismiss the user-centered mission, focusing instead on profit maximization.
- Share proprietary data with external competitors, compromising the company's innovation edge.

3. Strategic Considerations For Retention Or Removal

Retaining the Individual: A Path of Redemption

Jesus' decision to retain Judas, despite his eventual betrayal, suggests a belief in the possibility of redemption. By continuing to involve Judas in the mission, Jesus demonstrates:

- **Patience**: Allowing time for self-reflection and change.
- **Guidance**: Providing opportunities for the individual to realign with the mission.

Modern Application:

Leaders might choose to retain a potentially disloyal team member if:

- The individual shows signs of remorse or openness to feedback.
- The leader believes they can realign the person's goals with the organization's mission.
- The risk of harm can be mitigated through close monitoring or adjusted responsibilities.

Steps to Encourage Alignment:

1. **Open Dialogue**: Have candid conversations about the individual's behavior and its impact on the team.
2. **Clear Expectations**: Define specific, measurable goals for behavior and performance improvement.
3. **Mentorship**: Pair the individual with a trusted team member to model desired behaviors.

Removing the Individual: Protecting the Mission

In some cases, removal may be the only viable option. For example, Jesus ultimately allows Judas' betrayal to unfold, recognizing that it serves a greater purpose within His mission. While this decision aligns with His divine plan, it underscores the importance of timing and discernment in addressing betrayal.

Modern Application

Leaders might decide to remove a team member if:

- The individual's behavior poses a significant risk to the organization's goals or reputation.
- Efforts to realign their values have been unsuccessful.
- Their continued presence undermines team morale or trust.

Steps to Execute Removal Strategically:

1. **Document Concerns**: Maintain records of performance or behavioral issues to justify the decision.
2. **Communicate Transparently**: Clearly explain the reasons for the decision to the individual and, where appropriate, to the team.
3. **Minimize Disruption**: Plan for continuity by redistributing responsibilities and addressing team concerns.

4. Lessons For Modern Leaders

The story of Judas teaches modern leaders several critical lessons:

- **Discernment Matters**: Leaders must balance compassion with pragmatism, discerning whether an individual's potential outweighs the risks they pose.
- **Transparency Builds Resilience**: By being open about challenges, leaders can strengthen team trust and unity.
- **Sometimes, Letting Go is Necessary**: Removing a team member is difficult but may be essential to protect the mission and the team's well-being.

Practical Example
In a healthcare technology startup like *Health Empower*:

- If a team member undermines the mission by prioritizing profits over patient empowerment, the leader must decide whether mentorship or removal is the best course.
- Transparent communication about the decision, coupled with a focus on the organization's values, ensures the team remains aligned and motivated.

Protecting The Mission Without Sacrificing Integrity

The strategic conflict of handling a potential betrayer is one of the most challenging aspects of leadership. Jesus' example in the Gospel of Mark demonstrates the importance of balancing hope for redemption with the need to protect the mission. For modern leaders, this means making difficult decisions with clarity, compassion, and integrity.

By fostering open communication, addressing conflicts directly, and prioritizing the mission over personal discomfort, leaders can navigate these tensions effectively, ensuring their team remains focused, unified, and resilient in the face of challenges.

CHAPTER 3: SERVANT LEADERSHIP

◆ ◆ ◆

One of the most defining aspects of Jesus' leadership, as portrayed in the Gospel of Mark, is His radical commitment to servant leadership. Unlike the rulers and leaders of His time who often sought power, wealth, and control, Jesus turned the paradigm upside down, teaching that true greatness is found in serving others. In Mark 10:42-45, He declares, "Whoever wants to become great among you must be your servant, and whoever wants to be first must be slave of all. For even the Son of Man did not come to be served, but to serve, and to give His life as a ransom for many" (NIV).

Jesus' servant leadership as portrayed in the Gospel of Mark offers a countercultural yet profoundly effective model for modern leaders. By prioritizing the needs of others, balancing humility with authority, and leading by example, He created a team capable of carrying His mission forward into the world.

This chapter explores Jesus' philosophy of servant leadership, the tensions it creates with traditional views of authority, and how it applies to modern leadership contexts, particularly for startups and organizations seeking to drive meaningful change.

1. The Philosophy Of Servant Leadership

The Radical Shift from Power to Service

Jesus' model of leadership redefined greatness. Instead of exercising authority over others, as was common among rulers of the time, Jesus chose to lead by empowering and uplifting others. His life was a demonstration of this philosophy, from healing the sick to washing His disciples' feet.

Key Elements of Jesus' Servant Leadership

- **Empathy**: Jesus consistently demonstrated an ability to understand and respond to the needs of others. In Mark 6:34, He sees a large crowd and has compassion on them, "because they were like sheep without a shepherd."
- **Humility**: Jesus does not position Himself above others but works alongside them, meeting people at their level.
- **Sacrifice**: The ultimate expression of His servant leadership is His willingness to sacrifice Himself for the good of others, as described in Mark 10:45.

2. Tensions And Challenges Of Servant Leadership

Perceived Weakness

One common critique of servant leadership is the perception that it lacks authority or strength. Jesus faced similar criticisms.

In Mark 3:21, His family says, "He is out of His mind," and in Mark 15:31, religious leaders mock Him, saying, "He saved others, but He can't save Himself!" Yet, Jesus' ability to serve without needing to assert dominance reveals an inner strength that transforms those around Him.

Balancing Service and Authority

While Jesus led through service, He also demonstrated authority when necessary. For example:

- In Mark 4:39, He calms the storm with a command, showing His power over nature.
- In Mark 11:15-17, He drives out money changers from the temple, taking decisive action to uphold justice.

This balance is critical for leaders. Servant leadership does not mean passivity. Instead, it requires knowing when to serve and when to assert authority in service of the mission.

Modern Application

Startup leaders often face similar tensions. In a fast-paced environment, balancing humility and decisiveness is key:

- Leaders must empower their teams while maintaining accountability.
- Servant leadership doesn't mean avoiding difficult conversations or decisions but ensuring they are made with empathy and fairness.

3. Practical Expressions Of Servant Leadership

Meeting the Needs of the Team

In Mark 6:30-44, Jesus meets both the physical and spiritual needs of the crowd, feeding over 5,000 people with five loaves and two fish. This act demonstrates that servant leadership involves addressing immediate needs before asking for contributions or commitment.

Modern Application

Leaders can prioritize their team's well-being by:

- Providing resources and support to enable success (e.g., training, tools, or flexible work arrangements).
- Recognizing and addressing burnout or stress within the team.

Leading by Example

In Mark 9:35, Jesus says, "Anyone who wants to be first must be the very last, and the servant of all." He doesn't just teach this principle—He lives it, consistently putting others before Himself.

Modern Application

Leaders should model the behaviors they wish to see in their teams:

- **Accountability**: Take responsibility for failures and share credit for successes.
- **Work Ethic**: Demonstrate dedication to the mission, inspiring others through example.
- **Integrity**: Make decisions transparently and ethically.

Empowering Others to Lead

In Mark 6:7-13, Jesus sends His disciples out two by two, giving them authority to preach and heal. By empowering them, He multiplies His impact and prepares them for future leadership roles.

Modern Application

Empowering others is a cornerstone of servant leadership. Leaders can:

- Delegate meaningful responsibilities, allowing team members to grow.
- Invest in mentorship and professional development.
- Create an environment where ideas and initiatives are welcomed from all levels of the organization.

4. Servant Leadership In Startups And Mission-Driven Organizations

For startups, especially those with a mission-driven focus like *Health Empower*, servant leadership is not only an ethical choice but also a strategic one. Startups operate in uncertain, high-pressure environments where collaboration, trust, and innovation are crucial.

Benefits of Servant Leadership in Startups

- **Increased Team Engagement**: Employees are more likely to feel connected to a leader who prioritizes their growth and well-being.
- **Improved Innovation**: When leaders empower their teams, individuals are more likely to share ideas and take creative risks.
- **Resilience in Challenges**: A servant leader builds a culture of mutual support, enabling teams to weather setbacks and adapt to change.

Challenges to Implementing Servant Leadership

- **Time Pressure**: Startups often prioritize speed, which can make it challenging to invest time in relationship-building.
- **Perceived Lack of Authority**: Leaders may fear that prioritizing service will undermine their authority, especially in high-stakes situations.

Solutions:

- **Integrate Service into Strategy**: Align servant leadership principles with organizational goals, showing that they drive results.
- **Train for Leadership Balance**: Provide training for leaders to develop both empathetic and decisive leadership skills.

5. Lessons From Jesus For Modern Leaders

Serve Without Expecting Recognition

Jesus consistently served others without seeking acknowledgment or reward. This selflessness fosters trust and inspires others to follow.

Modern Application
Leaders can:

- Create systems for anonymous feedback, showing they value input over credit.
- Avoid micromanaging, trusting their team to achieve results.

Transform Through Service

By serving others, Jesus didn't just meet immediate needs— He transformed lives. Servant leaders today can create similar transformation by:

- Empowering employees to grow professionally and personally.
- Designing products or services that prioritize user needs and societal impact.

Leading By Serving

For startups and organizations like *Health Empower*, adopting servant leadership means not only inspiring and empowering teams but also creating a culture that drives innovation, resilience, and long-term impact. In the end, true greatness comes not from how many people serve you, but from how many lives you transform by serving them.

CHAPTER 4: TIME MANAGEMENT AND PRIORITIZATION

◆ ◆ ◆

Time is one of the most valuable resources a leader has, yet it is often the most difficult to manage effectively. In the Gospel of Mark, Jesus demonstrates an extraordinary ability to balance the demands of His mission with time for rest, reflection, and renewal. His approach offers timeless lessons on how leaders can prioritize effectively, manage competing demands, and remain focused on their vision without becoming overwhelmed.

This chapter explores Jesus' time management strategies as portrayed in Mark, the challenges He faced, and practical applications for leaders navigating the complexities of modern organizational life.

1. The Foundation Of Prioritization: A Clear Vision

Jesus' Mission-Centric Approach

From the outset of His ministry, Jesus exhibits a profound clarity about His mission. In Mark 1:38, He says, "Let us go somewhere else—to the nearby villages—so I can preach there also. That is why I have come." This clarity allows Him to make decisions about where to invest His time and energy, even when it means leaving behind pressing needs or expectations.

Modern Application

Leaders often face competing demands that can dilute their focus. A clear vision serves as a compass, helping them prioritize effectively. For example:

- **Align Decisions with Goals**: Before committing to tasks or projects, evaluate how they align with the organization's mission and long-term objectives.
- **Communicate Priorities**: Ensure that team members understand the vision so they can align their efforts and help maintain focus.

2. Balancing Action And Reflection

Jesus' Use of Solitude

Throughout Mark, Jesus frequently withdraws from the crowds to pray and reflect. In Mark 1:35, "Very early in the morning, while it was still dark, Jesus got up, left the house, and went off to a solitary place, where He prayed." This rhythm of action followed by reflection allows Him to maintain spiritual and emotional balance while staying connected to His mission.

The Tension Between Solitude and Demand

Even as Jesus seeks solitude, the demands of His ministry often interrupt Him. In Mark 1:36-37, the disciples find Him and say, "Everyone is looking for you!" Despite the constant pressure, Jesus returns to His mission with renewed focus.

Modern Application

Leaders, particularly in high-pressure environments like startups, often feel they cannot step away. However, moments of reflection are essential for sustained effectiveness. Strategies include:

- **Schedule Regular Reflection Time**: Block out time for strategic thinking, planning, or personal renewal.
- **Empower Delegation**: Build a team that can handle urgent matters in your absence, allowing you to step back without compromising operations.
- **Practice Mindfulness**: Incorporate practices like meditation or journaling to maintain clarity amidst competing demands.

3. Managing Interruptions And Staying Focused

Jesus' Flexibility in the Face of Interruptions

Despite His focus, Jesus demonstrates remarkable flexibility when interruptions align with His mission. In Mark 5:21-43, while on His way to heal Jairus' daughter, He stops to address a woman who touches His cloak for healing. Instead of dismissing the interruption, Jesus engages her, recognizing the importance of the moment.

Discernment in Addressing Needs

Not all interruptions receive the same response. In Mark 3:20-21, when His family tries to take charge of Him, believing He is "out of His mind," Jesus stays committed to His mission rather than acquiescing to their concerns. This discernment allows Him to manage interruptions without losing focus.

Modern Application

Leaders must navigate frequent interruptions while maintaining focus on their priorities. Practical strategies include:

- **Evaluate the Urgency and Relevance**: Assess whether an interruption requires immediate attention or can be addressed later.
- **Set Boundaries**: Communicate clearly with your team about when and how to approach you with issues.
- **Create Systems for Handling Interruptions**: Delegate certain types of decisions or problems to trusted team members to minimize distractions.

4. The Importance Of Rest And Renewal

Jesus' Commitment to Rest

In Mark 6:31, after the disciples return from their mission, Jesus tells them, "Come with me by yourselves to a quiet place and get some rest." This directive highlights Jesus' understanding that rest is essential for sustaining energy and focus, both for Himself and for His team.

Modern Application

Leaders who neglect rest often experience burnout, which

can diminish their effectiveness and harm their teams. Incorporating rest into a leadership routine involves:

- **Encouraging Work-Life Balance**: Promote a culture where team members feel empowered to rest and recharge.
- **Modeling Healthy Behavior**: Demonstrate the importance of rest by taking breaks yourself and respecting others' downtime.
- **Prioritizing Wellness**: Offer resources like wellness programs or flexible schedules to support the well-being of your team.

5. Delegation As A Time Management Strategy

Jesus' Empowerment of His Team

In Mark 6:7-13, Jesus sends His disciples out two by two, giving them authority to preach, heal, and cast out demons. By delegating responsibilities, He extends His mission's reach while conserving His own energy for strategic leadership.

Modern Application

Delegation is one of the most effective tools for managing time and multiplying impact. Leaders can:

- **Identify Opportunities for Delegation**: Focus on high-value tasks and entrust others with operational responsibilities.
- **Empower Team Members**: Provide the resources and authority needed for team members to take ownership of their roles.
- **Trust and Verify**: Allow others to lead while maintaining oversight to ensure alignment with organizational goals.

6. The Strategic Use Of Time For Long-Term

Impact

Jesus' Focus on Sustainable Growth

Jesus invests significant time in teaching His disciples, recognizing that they will carry His mission forward after His departure. In Mark 4:10-12, He explains the meaning of parables privately to His disciples, ensuring they understand His teachings deeply.

Modern Application

Leaders should balance short-term demands with long-term priorities, such as developing their team and preparing for future growth. Strategies include:

- **Investing in Team Development**: Offer training and mentorship to build skills and confidence within the team.
- **Focusing on Strategic Initiatives**: Allocate time for projects that have long-term benefits, even if they don't yield immediate results.
- **Building Succession Plans**: Prepare future leaders by involving them in strategic decision-making and leadership opportunities.

7. Lessons From Jesus For Modern Leaders

- **Clarify Your Mission**: Know your "why" and let it guide your time management decisions.
- **Balance Action and Reflection**: Incorporate regular moments of rest and reflection to maintain clarity and focus.
- **Embrace Flexibility**: Be open to interruptions when they align with your mission but practice discernment in addressing them.

- **Prioritize Rest**: Recognize that rest is not a luxury but a necessity for effective leadership.
- **Delegate Strategically**: Empower others to share responsibilities, freeing you to focus on your highest priorities.

Leading With Focus And Purpose

Time management is not simply about doing more in less time; it's about doing the right things at the right time. Jesus' approach to prioritization in the Gospel of Mark demonstrates that effective leadership requires a balance of focus, flexibility, and intentionality. By applying these principles, modern leaders can navigate competing demands, sustain their energy, and remain true to their vision, ensuring long-term success and impact.

CHAPTER 5: COMMUNICATION SKILLS

◆ ◆ ◆

One of the most remarkable aspects of Jesus' leadership, as portrayed in the Gospel of Mark, is His ability to communicate effectively with diverse audiences. From His intimate conversations with the disciples to His public teachings to large crowds, Jesus consistently conveys His message with clarity, authority, and empathy. His communication style is deeply purposeful, blending simplicity with depth and truth with grace. In this chapter, we explore the principles, techniques, and strategies Jesus used to communicate and their relevance for modern leaders.

1. The Power Of Storytelling

Jesus' Use of Parables

In Mark 4:1-20, Jesus teaches the Parable of the Sower to a large crowd. This parable, like many others, uses familiar agricultural imagery to convey profound spiritual truths. Jesus deliberately chooses storytelling as a method to engage listeners, provoke thought, and communicate complex ideas in relatable ways.

Why Stories Work

- **Emotional Connection**: Stories resonate with people on an emotional level, making abstract concepts tangible.
- **Memorability**: Stories are easier to remember than facts or instructions.
- **Engagement**: A well-told story captivates attention and invites participation.

Modern Application

Leaders can harness the power of storytelling to:

- Illustrate the vision and mission of their organization.
- Inspire teams during challenging times by sharing success stories.
- Simplify complex ideas to make them accessible to stakeholders or customers.

Practical Example

A healthcare technology startup like *Health Empower* might use patient stories to demonstrate the platform's impact, helping stakeholders connect emotionally with the company's mission.

2. Clarity And Simplicity

Speaking with Simplicity

Jesus often simplifies profound truths to ensure they are understandable. For example, in Mark 12:30-31, He distills the greatest commandments into two simple principles: love God and love your neighbor. This ability to distill complex ideas into actionable insights makes His teachings accessible to all.

Avoiding Overcomplication

In Mark 4:33-34, Jesus teaches the crowds in parables but explains everything privately to His disciples. This dual approach ensures clarity for both general audiences and those who require deeper understanding.

Modern Application:

Leaders often face the challenge of communicating with multiple stakeholders—teams, investors, customers, and partners. Strategies include:

- Avoiding jargon and using language that resonates with the audience.
- Tailoring communication to different groups while maintaining consistency in the core message.
- Encouraging questions to ensure understanding.

Practical Example:

When presenting a new feature of *Health Empower* to users, the team might simplify its explanation to emphasize ease of use and benefits while offering detailed documentation for more technical audiences.

3. Listening As A Key Communication Skill

Jesus' Attentive Listening

In Mark 10:46-52, Jesus encounters Bartimaeus, a blind beggar. When Bartimaeus calls out to Him, Jesus asks, "What do you want me to do for you?" This question demonstrates Jesus' willingness to listen deeply, even when the need might seem obvious. By listening, He validates Bartimaeus' voice and empowers him to express his need.

Empathy Through Listening

Jesus' ability to listen fosters trust and connection. It shows that He values individuals, not just the larger mission.

Modern Application

Effective leaders are not only great speakers but also active listeners. Strategies include:

- Asking open-ended questions to understand team members' perspectives.
- Practicing reflective listening to ensure understanding.
- Creating safe spaces for feedback and dialogue.

Practical Example:

A leader at *Health Empower* might hold regular one-on-one meetings with team members to listen to their challenges and ideas, fostering a culture of mutual respect and innovation.

4. Adapting To The Audience

Jesus' Versatility in Communication

Jesus tailors His message to suit different audiences.

- To the crowds, He uses parables and simple analogies (Mark 4:1-20).
- To the disciples, He provides deeper explanations (Mark 4:34).
- To critics, such as the Pharisees, He responds with sharp logic and scripture-based arguments (Mark 12:13-17).

Knowing Your Audience

Jesus' ability to read the room allows Him to communicate

effectively, regardless of the audience's background or motives.

Modern Application:
Leaders must adapt their communication style based on the audience's needs and context. Strategies include:

- Using data-driven presentations for analytical stakeholders.
- Focusing on emotional and personal connections with customers or end-users.
- Being direct and solution-focused when addressing team challenges.

Practical Example:
When pitching *Health Empower* to investors, leaders might emphasize metrics and ROI. When engaging users, the focus might shift to personal empowerment and ease of use.

5. Communicating With Authority

Jesus' Confidence and Credibility

In Mark 1:22, people are amazed at Jesus' teaching because "He taught them as one who had authority, not as the teachers of the law." Jesus' authority comes from His knowledge, conviction, and alignment with His mission.

Combining Authority with Humility

While Jesus speaks with authority, He also demonstrates humility, making His message more relatable and inspiring.

Modern Application:
Leaders must balance authority with humility to inspire trust and confidence. Strategies include:

- Speaking confidently about the organization's mission and values.
- Backing up claims with evidence and results.

- Acknowledging areas of uncertainty or seeking input from others.

Practical Example:
A leader at *Health Empower* might confidently articulate the platform's potential while inviting user feedback to improve its features.

6. Addressing Criticism And Opposition

Jesus' Responses to Critics

In Mark 12:13-17, Jesus is asked whether it is lawful to pay taxes to Caesar—a question designed to trap Him. His response, "Give back to Caesar what is Caesar's and to God what is God's," is both brilliant and disarming. He defuses the tension while remaining true to His principles.

Grace Under Pressure

Jesus consistently handles criticism with grace and wisdom, turning challenges into opportunities to clarify His mission.

Modern Application:
Leaders often face criticism, whether from competitors, customers, or internal stakeholders. Strategies include:

- Staying calm and composed under pressure.
- Acknowledging valid points while reframing the conversation to align with the mission.
- Using criticism as a tool for growth and improvement.

Practical Example:
If *Health Empower* faces criticism about data privacy, the leadership team might respond by emphasizing its robust privacy measures and inviting external audits to validate its

claims.

7. Inspiring Through Vision

Jesus' Visionary Communication

Jesus consistently communicates a compelling vision of the Kingdom of God. In Mark 1:15, He declares, "The time has come... The Kingdom of God has come near. Repent and believe the good news!" This vision inspires hope and calls for action, motivating His followers to join His mission.

The Call to Action

Jesus combines vision with practical steps, such as repentance, faith, and love, making it actionable for His audience.

Modern Application

Leaders can inspire their teams and stakeholders by:

- Painting a clear picture of the organization's future.
- Connecting the vision to individual roles and contributions.
- Celebrating progress toward the vision to maintain momentum.

Practical Example

A *Health Empower* leader might articulate a vision of a world where everyone can manage their health independently, emphasizing how each team member's work contributes to achieving this goal.

Communicating With Purpose And Power

Jesus' communication style in the Gospel of Mark offers profound lessons for modern leaders. His ability to connect with diverse audiences, convey complex truths simply, and inspire action provides a blueprint for effective leadership communication.

For leaders in mission-driven organizations like *Health Empower*, adopting these principles—storytelling, clarity, listening, adaptability, authority, and vision—can enhance their ability to connect, inspire, and lead. In the end, communication is not just about transferring information; it's about building trust, fostering understanding, and empowering others to join the mission.

CHAPTER 6: HANDLING OPPOSITION AND CONFLICT

◆ ◆ ◆

No leader, regardless of their mission, escapes opposition and conflict. The Gospel of Mark vividly portrays Jesus' encounters with critics, skeptics, and outright adversaries. From religious leaders challenging His authority to misunderstandings within His own circle, Jesus faced continual opposition yet responded with wisdom, grace, and unwavering focus on His mission.

The Socio-Political Landscape of Judea

Historical Context

Opposition is a defining aspect of leadership, but understanding its roots and dynamics is essential for responding effectively. In the Gospel of Mark, Jesus faces consistent opposition from religious leaders, Roman authorities, and even His followers. This chapter delves into the socio-political and cultural context of Roman-occupied Judea to provide a richer understanding of the challenges Jesus navigated and the strategies He employed. By situating Jesus' leadership within His historical context, we uncover deeper lessons on addressing opposition with wisdom, grace, and courage.

Roman Occupation

Judea in the first century was under Roman rule, marked by heavy taxation, military oversight, and limited autonomy. Roman authorities enforced a system of control that demanded loyalty to Caesar while allowing some religious freedom. This arrangement created tension, particularly for devout Jews who resented Roman intrusion into their spiritual and national identity.

Religious Fragmentation

The Jewish population was divided into several sects:

- **Pharisees**: Religious leaders focused on strict adherence to the law, often clashing with Jesus over interpretations of scripture and tradition.
- **Sadducees**: An elite group aligned with Roman authorities, focused on maintaining power and control through cooperation.
- **Zealots**: A radical faction advocating armed resistance against Rome.
- **Common People**: Often impoverished and oppressed, this group looked to religious leaders or messianic figures for hope.

These divisions created a volatile environment where Jesus'

teachings and actions were scrutinized from all sides.

In this chapter, we explore how Jesus navigated opposition and conflict, balancing truth and compassion, and how modern leaders can apply these principles in navigating the challenges they face.

1. Identifying Sources Of Opposition

The Nature of Jesus' Opposition

In Mark, Jesus faces resistance from multiple fronts:

- **Religious Leaders**: Pharisees and scribes challenge His teachings, questioning His authority (Mark 2:6-7, Mark 3:22).
- **Cultural Expectations**: Jesus' approach to traditions, such as healing on the Sabbath (Mark 3:1-6), disrupts societal norms.
- **Personal Relationships**: Even Jesus' own family doubts Him, believing He is out of His mind (Mark 3:21).

Why Opposition Arises

Opposition often stems from fear of change, perceived threats to power, or misunderstanding of the mission. For Jesus, His revolutionary message of love, grace, and the Kingdom of God disrupted deeply entrenched systems of control and tradition.

Modern Application

Leaders today encounter opposition from:

- Internal stakeholders resistant to organizational change.
- Competitors threatened by innovative ideas.
- Misunderstandings among team members or customers.

By understanding the root causes of opposition, leaders can address it effectively rather than reactively.

2. Responding To Criticism With Clarity And Calm

Jesus' Composed Responses

In Mark 12:13-17, the Pharisees and Herodians attempt to trap Jesus with the question of paying taxes to Caesar. Instead of being provoked, Jesus responds with wisdom: "Give back to Caesar what is Caesar's and to God what is God's." His reply not only disarms the critics but also reinforces His mission without compromise.

Staying Calm Under Pressure

Jesus' ability to remain calm stems from His clarity of purpose and confidence in His mission. He doesn't react emotionally but responds thoughtfully, often reframing the issue to focus on deeper truths.

Modern Application

Leaders can respond to criticism by:

- Remaining composed and avoiding emotional reactions.
- Listening actively to understand the underlying concerns.
- Framing responses in a way that aligns with the organization's mission and values.

Practical Example

If a healthcare startup like *Health Empower* faces skepticism about its ability to disrupt traditional healthcare systems, leaders could respond by emphasizing the platform's benefits while inviting constructive dialogue with critics.

3. Choosing Battles Wisely

Jesus' Strategic Silence

Not every challenge requires a response. In Mark 14:61, when Jesus is on trial before the Sanhedrin, He remains silent in the face of false accusations. His silence reflects discernment, choosing not to engage in arguments that would detract from His purpose.

Focusing on the Bigger Picture

Jesus demonstrates an ability to prioritize, addressing opposition only when it serves the mission. This focus prevents Him from being distracted by every challenge or criticism.

Modern Application

Leaders must decide when to engage and when to let opposition pass. Strategies include:

- Assessing whether addressing the conflict advances the mission.
- Avoiding reactive responses to criticism that lack substance or relevance.
- Prioritizing high-impact issues over trivial disagreements.

Practical Example

A leader at *Health Empower* might choose to ignore minor public criticisms on social media while addressing significant concerns raised by regulatory agencies.

4. Balancing Truth And Grace

Jesus' Compassionate Confrontations

In Mark 2:23-28, Jesus defends His disciples for picking grain on the Sabbath, saying, "The Sabbath was made for man, not man for the Sabbath." While confronting the Pharisees' legalism, Jesus communicates with grace, reframing the issue to focus on the underlying principle of compassion.

Correcting Without Condemning

Jesus addresses opposition firmly yet compassionately, ensuring His message remains transformative rather than alienating.

Modern Application

Leaders can balance truth and grace by:

- Addressing conflicts directly but with empathy and respect.
- Acknowledging valid concerns while standing firm on core principles.
- Seeking solutions that align with organizational values rather than escalating tensions.

Practical Example

If a team member at *Health Empower* resists a new process due to fear of change, a leader might empathize with their concerns while explaining the benefits and providing support for the transition.

5. Turning Opposition Into Opportunity

Jesus' Use of Conflict for Teaching

In Mark 3:1-6, Jesus heals a man with a withered hand on the Sabbath, knowing it will provoke the Pharisees. He uses the moment to ask, "Which is lawful on the Sabbath: to do good or to do evil, to save life or to kill?" This rhetorical question turns the opposition into an opportunity to clarify His mission and challenge legalistic traditions.

Reframing Criticism

Jesus often reframes opposition as a chance to teach and inspire others, focusing not on the attack but on the lesson it presents.

Modern Application: Leaders can use opposition as an opportunity to:

- Clarify the organization's mission and goals.
- Strengthen team unity by addressing challenges together.
- Innovate and improve in response to constructive criticism.

Practical Example

If stakeholders criticize *Health Empower* for bypassing traditional healthcare systems, leaders could use the opportunity to showcase how the platform complements existing systems while empowering individuals.

6. Building Resilience Through Opposition

Jesus' Resilience in the Face of Betrayal

In Mark 14:43-46, Jesus is betrayed by Judas, one of His own disciples. Despite the personal pain of betrayal, Jesus remains focused on His mission, refusing to retaliate or abandon His purpose.

The Role of Perseverance

Jesus' ability to endure opposition without losing sight of His mission is a testament to His resilience. His example encourages leaders to remain steadfast, even in the face of significant challenges.

Modern Application

Leaders can build resilience by:

- Developing a clear sense of purpose that sustains them through difficulties.
- Learning from setbacks rather than becoming discouraged.
- Surrounding themselves with a supportive team to share the burden of leadership.

Practical Example

If internal conflicts arise at *Health Empower*, a resilient leader might focus on reaffirming the team's shared vision and resolving the conflict collaboratively rather than letting it derail progress.

7. Lessons For Modern Leaders

Key Takeaways from Jesus' Approach to Conflict

- **Clarity of Mission**: A clear sense of purpose helps leaders navigate opposition without losing focus.
- **Discernment**: Not every challenge requires engagement; choose battles wisely.
- **Composure**: Staying calm under pressure builds credibility and trust.
- **Empathy**: Addressing conflicts with compassion fosters understanding and resolution.

- **Resilience**: Opposition is inevitable; perseverance ensures long-term success.

Practical Strategies for Modern Leaders

1. **Anticipate Opposition**: Prepare for resistance by identifying potential sources and addressing concerns proactively.
2. **Foster Open Dialogue**: Create an environment where team members and stakeholders feel comfortable raising issues.
3. **Turn Criticism into Growth**: Use opposition as a catalyst for innovation and improvement.

Navigating Opposition With Wisdom And Grace

Opposition and conflict are inevitable in leadership, but how leaders respond defines their effectiveness. Jesus' example in the Gospel of Mark demonstrates the power of balancing truth and grace, remaining composed under pressure, and using opposition as an opportunity to clarify and strengthen the mission.

For modern leaders, especially those in mission-driven organizations like *Health Empower*, these principles provide a roadmap for navigating challenges with wisdom, resilience, and integrity. By handling opposition effectively, leaders not only protect their mission but also build trust, inspire loyalty, and create opportunities for transformation.

CHAPTER 7:
DELEGATION
AND TRUST

◆ ◆ ◆

L eadership is not about doing everything yourself; it's about empowering others to share in the mission. Delegation is one of the most critical aspects of leadership, yet it is also one of the most challenging to execute effectively. In the Gospel of Mark, Jesus models a masterful approach to delegation, entrusting His disciples with significant responsibilities while providing guidance and support. This chapter explores how Jesus delegated tasks, the principles He applied, and how leaders can cultivate trust while empowering their teams.

1. The Purpose Of Delegation

Jesus' Vision for Multiplication

Jesus understood that the scope of His mission—to proclaim the Kingdom of God—was too vast to accomplish alone. In Mark 6:7-13, He sends the twelve disciples out two by two, giving them authority to preach, heal, and drive out demons. This act of delegation not only expanded His reach but also prepared the disciples for future leadership.

Benefits of Delegation

- **Scalability**: By empowering others, leaders can extend the impact of their mission.
- **Team Development**: Delegation allows team members to grow in confidence, skills, and leadership capacity.
- **Focus on Strategic Priorities**: Leaders can devote their time to high-level decisions and vision-setting.

Modern Application

In a startup like *Health Empower*, delegation is essential for scaling operations. Leaders must recognize that empowering their team not only distributes workload but also fosters innovation and ownership.

2. Principles Of Effective Delegation

Authority and Responsibility

Jesus delegates not just tasks but authority, empowering His disciples to act in His name. In Mark 6:7, He gives them authority over impure spirits, trusting them to carry out their mission without direct oversight.

Key Principle: Delegation is most effective when team members are given the authority to make decisions within their responsibilities.

Modern Application

- Clearly define the scope of authority for each role.
- Ensure team members understand their decision-making boundaries.
- Trust individuals to act without micromanagement, while remaining available for guidance.

Clarity in Instructions

Before sending out His disciples, Jesus provides clear instructions: take nothing for the journey except a staff—no bread, no bag, no money (Mark 6:8-9). These guidelines ensure the disciples focus on their mission without unnecessary distractions.

Key Principle: Effective delegation requires clear communication of expectations, objectives, and resources.

Modern Application

- Provide detailed briefs for tasks or projects, outlining goals, timelines, and resources.
- Use tools like project management software to track progress and ensure alignment.
- Regularly check in to address questions or challenges.

Support and Feedback

Though Jesus sends His disciples out independently, He remains their point of reference and later debriefs with them. In Mark 6:30, the disciples return to Jesus and report on their work, allowing Him to provide feedback and encouragement.

Key Principle: Delegation is not abdication. Leaders must remain engaged and provide constructive feedback to support their team.

Modern Application

- Hold regular one-on-one meetings to review progress and provide mentorship.
- Celebrate successes to build confidence and morale.
- Address areas for improvement with a growth-oriented mindset.

3. Building Trust Through Delegation

Jesus' Trust in His Disciples

Despite their lack of experience, Jesus entrusts His disciples with critical tasks. This trust is evident when He allows them to represent Him publicly and perform miracles in His name. His confidence in them inspires their confidence in themselves.

Key Principle: Trust is the foundation of successful delegation. Leaders must believe in their team's ability to deliver.

Modern Application:

- **Start Small**: Assign manageable tasks to build trust gradually.
- **Empower Decision-Making**: Encourage team members to propose solutions and take initiative.
- **Acknowledge Growth**: Recognize and reward team members who demonstrate competence and accountability.

Managing Fear of Failure

Trusting others can be daunting, especially when the stakes are high. Jesus demonstrates that failure is an opportunity for growth. For example, in Mark 9:14-29, when the disciples fail to cast out a demon, Jesus uses the moment to teach them about the importance of prayer.

Key Principle: Embrace failure as a learning opportunity rather than a setback.

Modern Application:

- Create a culture where mistakes are seen as opportunities for improvement.
- Debrief after challenges to identify lessons learned and prevent future issues.
- Offer support rather than criticism when team members encounter difficulties.

4. Delegation In High-Stakes Situations

Jesus' Delegation in Feeding the 5,000

In Mark 6:35-44, Jesus involves His disciples in the miracle of feeding the 5,000. Though He performs the multiplication of loaves and fish, He delegates the tasks of organizing the crowd and distributing food to the disciples. This collaboration reinforces their role in His mission.

Key Principle: Even in high-stakes situations, delegation strengthens team cohesion and capability.

Modern Application:

- Break down large, complex projects into manageable tasks that can be delegated.
- Assign roles based on team members' strengths and expertise.

- Maintain oversight without taking over, ensuring the team feels empowered to succeed.

5. The Long-Term Impact Of Delegation

Preparing for Succession

Jesus' delegation is not just about sharing the workload—it's about preparing His disciples for future leadership. In Mark 16:15-20, after His resurrection, He commissions them to continue His mission, demonstrating the trust He has built over time.

Key Principle: Delegation is a tool for leadership development and succession planning.

Modern Application:

- Invest in training and mentorship to prepare team members for leadership roles.
- Identify high-potential employees and provide opportunities for them to lead.
- Create a succession plan to ensure organizational continuity.

6. Overcoming Barriers To Delegation

Common Challenges

- **Fear of Losing Control**: Leaders may hesitate to delegate, worrying that tasks won't be done correctly.
- **Lack of Trust**: Without confidence in their team, leaders may avoid delegation.
- **Micromanagement**: Hovering over tasks undermines the purpose of delegation.

Modern Application: Leaders can overcome these barriers by:

1. **Building a Culture of Accountability**: Set clear expectations and hold team members responsible for their results.
2. **Developing Communication Skills**: Ensure open channels for questions, updates, and feedback.
3. **Letting Go of Perfection**: Focus on results rather than rigid adherence to personal methods.

7. Lessons For Modern Leaders

- **Delegate Authority, Not Just Tasks**: Empower team members to make decisions and take ownership.
- **Provide Clear Instructions**: Ensure everyone understands the goals and resources available.
- **Trust and Verify**: Build trust while maintaining oversight to ensure alignment with the mission.
- **Embrace Mistakes**: Use failures as opportunities for growth and learning.
- **Prepare for the Future**: Use delegation to develop the next generation of leaders.

Conclusion: Empowering Others To Multiply Impact

Delegation is not just a practical necessity; it's a strategic tool for empowering others and multiplying impact. Jesus' approach in the Gospel of Mark demonstrates that effective delegation requires trust, clarity, and a willingness to let others grow through experience.

For modern leaders, particularly those in mission-driven organizations like *Health Empower*, these principles provide a roadmap for building capable teams and sustaining long-term success. By delegating effectively, leaders can focus on their highest priorities, foster innovation, and prepare their teams to carry the mission forward.

When Delegation Goes Wrong

D elegation, while essential for effective leadership, does not always yield the desired results. Even the best leaders experience setbacks when tasks are delegated. In the Gospel of Mark, Jesus encounters moments where His disciples fall short of expectations. These instances provide valuable insights into how leaders can navigate the challenges of delegation, address failures constructively, and refine their approach to empower their teams more effectively.

1. Recognizing When Delegation Fails

Failure in Execution

In Mark 9:14-29, Jesus' disciples attempt to cast out a demon but fail, leading to public embarrassment and criticism. The disciples are confused and frustrated, asking Jesus privately, "Why couldn't we drive it out?" (Mark 9:28). Jesus' response highlights a lack of preparation: "This kind can come out only by prayer."

Misalignment with the Mission

Delegation can also go wrong when team members act contrary to the mission. For instance, in Mark 10:35-37, James and John request positions of power in Jesus' Kingdom, misunderstanding the nature of servant leadership. Their actions create tension among the disciples, illustrating how a lack of alignment can disrupt team dynamics.

Modern Application

Delegation fails for several reasons:

- **Lack of Clarity**: Team members are unsure of the objectives or expectations.
- **Insufficient Preparation**: Delegated individuals lack the necessary skills, resources, or support.
- **Misaligned Values**: The task is approached in a way that conflicts with the organization's mission or culture.

By identifying these pitfalls, leaders can address issues proactively and reduce the likelihood of failure.

2. Responding Constructively To Delegation Failures

Jesus' Approach: Teaching Moments

When the disciples fail to cast out the demon, Jesus does not condemn them. Instead, He uses the moment as a teaching opportunity, emphasizing the importance of preparation and prayer. His response redirects their frustration into a learning experience, equipping them for future success.

Balancing Accountability and Support

In Mark 9:19, Jesus expresses frustration, saying, "You unbelieving generation... how long shall I stay with you?" Yet, He follows this with action, healing the boy and explaining the lesson to His disciples privately. This balance between accountability and support strengthens the disciples' growth.

Modern Application

Leaders can turn delegation failures into opportunities for growth:

- **Debrief After Failures**: Hold a constructive discussion to identify what went wrong and how to improve.
- **Provide Additional Training**: Equip team members with the skills and resources needed for similar tasks in the future.
- **Encourage Resilience**: Frame failures as a natural part of growth, fostering a culture of continuous improvement.

Example: If a team at *Health Empower* misses a deadline for a critical feature rollout, the leader might hold a retrospective to analyze bottlenecks and adjust processes, ensuring the team is better prepared for the next project.

3. Addressing Misalignment

Jesus' Realignment of Values

When James and John request positions of power, Jesus redirects their ambition toward servant leadership, saying, "Whoever wants to become great among you must be your servant" (Mark 10:43). He takes the opportunity to clarify the values of His mission, ensuring the disciples understand the importance of humility and service.

The Danger of Misaligned Delegation

When team members pursue personal goals that conflict with organizational priorities, the entire mission can be jeopardized. Misaligned delegation can result in:

- Erosion of trust within the team.
- Wasted resources and time.

- Potential damage to the organization's reputation.

Modern Application

Leaders can prevent and address misalignment by:

1. **Reinforcing Core Values**: Regularly communicate the organization's mission and values to ensure alignment.
2. **Setting Clear Boundaries**: Define acceptable methods and behaviors for achieving goals.
3. **Intervening Early**: Address signs of misalignment quickly to prevent escalation.

Example: If a marketing lead at *Health Empower* prioritizes flashy campaigns over user-centered messaging, the leader might hold a values alignment session to refocus efforts on the organization's mission to empower individuals in healthcare.

4. Preparing For Delegation Success

Jesus' Emphasis on Preparation

Before sending out the twelve disciples, Jesus equips them with clear instructions and authority (Mark 6:7-13). He sets boundaries—what to take, how to respond to rejection—and provides them with a framework for success.

The Cost of Insufficient Preparation

When the disciples fail to cast out the demon, the underlying issue is a lack of readiness. Jesus highlights that certain challenges require deeper spiritual preparation, underscoring the importance of equipping team members for the tasks they face.

Modern Application

To prevent delegation failures, leaders should:

- **Invest in Training**: Ensure team members have the knowledge and skills required for their roles.
- **Provide Resources**: Equip individuals with the tools and support they need to succeed.
- **Simulate Scenarios**: Offer low-risk opportunities for team members to practice and refine their abilities before tackling high-stakes tasks.

Example: Before assigning a junior developer at *Health Empower* to lead a project, the leader might pair them with a mentor or provide mock scenarios to build confidence and competence.

5. Recognizing When To Reassign Tasks

Jesus' Awareness of Team Limitations

While Jesus delegates extensively, He also recognizes the limitations of His disciples. In Mark 9:16-29, after the disciples fail to cast out the demon, Jesus intervenes personally. This demonstrates that delegation does not mean abdication; leaders must remain ready to step in when necessary.

Criteria for Reassignment

Delegation may need to be adjusted when:

- A task exceeds the current capabilities of the team member.
- The individual's approach consistently conflicts with organizational values.
- The stakes are too high for learning through failure.

Modern Application

Reassigning tasks should be handled with sensitivity to maintain trust and morale:

- **Frame It as a Partnership**: Offer additional support rather than outright removal.
- **Communicate the Decision Clearly**: Explain the rationale for reassignment while affirming confidence in the individual's potential.
- **Provide Growth Opportunities**: Ensure the team member has a path to regain responsibilities as they develop their skills.

Example: If a product manager at *Health Empower* struggles with coordinating a high-profile launch, the leader might temporarily assign a senior mentor to co-manage the project, ensuring success while fostering growth.

6. Learning From Delegation Failures

Jesus' Long-Term Perspective

Despite moments of failure, Jesus remains committed to His disciples' development. He understands that their growth will enable them to carry the mission forward after His departure. In Mark 16:15-20, the disciples, once faltering, are commissioned to lead the global mission—a testament to the transformative power of persistence and mentorship.

Modern Application

Leaders can learn from delegation failures by:

- **Conducting Post-Mortems**: Analyze what went wrong and

identify systemic improvements.

- **Adjusting Strategies**: Refine delegation processes based on lessons learned.
- **Maintaining Long-Term Focus**: View setbacks as stepping stones in the team's overall development.

7. Lessons For Modern Leaders

When delegation goes wrong, it's not a sign of failure but an opportunity to improve processes, communication, and trust. Key lessons include:

1. **Prepare Thoroughly**: Equip team members with the skills, resources, and guidance they need to succeed.
2. **Stay Involved**: Delegation requires ongoing support and feedback.
3. **Learn from Setbacks**: Use failures as opportunities to grow individually and collectively.
4. **Maintain Trust**: Handle reassignment or correction with empathy to preserve relationships and morale.
5. **Focus on Long-Term Impact**: Keep the bigger picture in mind, knowing that short-term challenges can lead to long-term growth.

Refining Delegation Through Challenges

Delegation, while essential, is rarely perfect. Jesus' experiences in the Gospel of Mark show that even the most skilled leader encounters challenges when empowering others. What sets great leaders apart is their ability to respond constructively, using failures as opportunities for growth and improvement.

For modern leaders, especially those in mission-driven organizations like *Health Empower*, refining delegation is an ongoing process. By preparing thoroughly, addressing misalignments, and maintaining trust, leaders can turn delegation setbacks into catalysts for transformation, building stronger teams and achieving greater impact.

CHAPTER 8:
INNOVATION AND
ADAPTABILITY

◆ ◆ ◆

L eadership requires not only a clear vision but also the ability to innovate and adapt in the face of changing circumstances. In the Gospel of Mark, Jesus exemplifies both innovation and adaptability in how He communicates His mission, addresses challenges, and interacts with diverse audiences. His actions consistently reflect a willingness to challenge the status quo, introduce new paradigms, and adjust His approach without compromising His core values.

This chapter explores the principles of innovation and adaptability as modeled by Jesus in the Gospel of Mark, focusing on how leaders can apply these lessons in modern contexts to navigate uncertainty, foster creativity, and drive meaningful change.

1. Challenging The Status Quo

Jesus as a Disruptor

Jesus' teachings and actions often challenge established norms and traditions. In Mark 2:18-22, when questioned about why His disciples do not fast like the Pharisees, He responds, "No one sews a patch of unshrunk cloth on an old garment... And no one pours new wine into old wineskins." This metaphor highlights the incompatibility of His revolutionary message with outdated systems, signaling a need for change.

The Cost of Innovation

Jesus' willingness to challenge the status quo often invites opposition. For example, His healing on the Sabbath (Mark 3:1-6) angers religious leaders, who begin plotting against Him. Yet, He remains resolute, prioritizing the well-being of people over rigid adherence to tradition.

Modern Application

Leaders in innovative industries often face resistance when introducing new ideas. Strategies for challenging the status quo include:

- **Clearly Articulating the Why**: Communicate the rationale behind changes to gain buy-in.
- **Demonstrating Value**: Use small wins to showcase the benefits of new approaches.
- **Balancing Tradition and Innovation**: Respect existing systems while advocating for necessary change.

Practical Example: In a healthcare startup like *Health Empower*, leaders might face skepticism from traditional healthcare providers. By emphasizing how the platform complements existing systems and improves patient outcomes, leaders can navigate resistance while driving innovation.

2. Embracing Flexibility In Execution

Jesus' Adaptive Ministry

Throughout Mark, Jesus demonstrates remarkable adaptability in how He executes His mission. He tailors His approach based on the needs of the moment:

- **With the Crowds**: He teaches in parables to simplify complex truths (Mark 4:1-20).
- **With the Disciples**: He provides deeper explanations, preparing them for leadership (Mark 4:34).
- **With Individuals**: He personalizes His interactions, such as healing the hemorrhaging woman with compassion and direct engagement (Mark 5:25-34).

The Role of Context

Jesus' ability to adapt reflects His understanding of context. Whether speaking to fishermen, religious leaders, or marginalized individuals, He meets people where they are, making His message relevant and accessible.

Modern Application

Adaptability is crucial for leaders navigating dynamic environments. Strategies include:

- **Listening to Feedback**: Stay attuned to the needs and concerns of stakeholders.
- **Iterating Quickly**: Use agile methodologies to test, learn, and refine solutions.
- **Customizing Approaches**: Tailor strategies to different

audiences while maintaining consistency in values.

Practical Example: A leader at *Health Empower* might use patient testimonials to connect emotionally with end-users, while presenting data and ROI metrics to appeal to investors.

3. Encouraging Creativity And Innovation

Jesus' Innovative Teachings

Jesus often employs creative methods to convey His message. In Mark 12:13-17, He turns a trap question about paying taxes into a profound teaching, saying, "Give back to Caesar what is Caesar's and to God what is God's." His ability to think on His feet not only diffuses the conflict but also leaves His audience with a transformative insight.

Fostering Creativity Among Followers

Jesus encourages His disciples to think creatively, such as when they face logistical challenges. In the feeding of the 5,000 (Mark 6:35-44), He involves the disciples in finding a solution, challenging them to think beyond conventional limitations.

Modern Application: Leaders can foster a culture of creativity by:

- **Encouraging Experimentation**: Create an environment where team members feel safe to propose and test new ideas.
- **Involving the Team in Problem-Solving**: Empower employees to take ownership of challenges and contribute

solutions.

- **Recognizing Innovative Thinking**: Celebrate creative contributions to reinforce their value.

Practical Example: At *Health Empower*, leaders might host hackathons or brainstorming sessions to generate innovative features for the platform, leveraging diverse perspectives to drive creativity.

4. Balancing Consistency With Innovation

Jesus' Core Values

While Jesus frequently innovates, He remains consistent in His core values. His actions, whether healing, teaching, or confronting opposition, are always aligned with His mission to proclaim the Kingdom of God and serve others.

The Danger of Over-Innovation

Unrestrained innovation can dilute focus and confuse stakeholders. Jesus avoids this by grounding His actions in a clear purpose, ensuring that His innovations enhance rather than detract from His mission.

Modern Application

Leaders should strike a balance between innovation and consistency:

- **Define Non-Negotiables**: Establish core values and principles that guide decision-making.
- **Align Innovation with Goals**: Ensure new initiatives support the organization's mission.
- **Communicate Continuity**: Reassure stakeholders that innovation complements, rather than replaces, existing

strengths.

Practical Example: While introducing AI-driven diagnostics, *Health Empower* leaders might emphasize that the technology enhances patient autonomy without replacing the role of healthcare professionals.

5. Leading Through Change

Jesus' Example in Transition

Jesus prepares His disciples for change by gradually transitioning leadership responsibilities. In Mark 6:7-13, He sends them out two by two, allowing them to practice and learn while still under His guidance. This gradual approach equips them for their eventual independent roles.

The Role of Communication

Throughout the Gospel of Mark, Jesus consistently communicates the bigger picture, helping His followers understand how individual actions contribute to the larger mission. This foresight eases the discomfort of change and builds trust.

Modern Application: Leading change requires clear communication and intentional planning:

- **Involve the Team Early**: Engage stakeholders in the change process to build ownership.
- **Communicate the Vision**: Connect changes to the organization's mission and long-term goals.
- **Provide Support**: Offer training and resources to help teams navigate transitions.

Practical Example: If *Health Empower* shifts focus to global markets, leaders might involve team members in market research, communicate the strategic importance of the move, and provide cross-cultural training to ensure a smooth transition.

6. Innovating For Long-Term Impact

Jesus' Legacy of Innovation

Jesus' willingness to innovate creates a foundation for lasting impact. His use of parables, redefinition of traditions, and empowerment of His disciples ensure that His message continues to influence generations.

Building for Sustainability

Jesus invests in people, prioritizing discipleship and teaching to ensure that His mission outlives His earthly ministry. This focus on sustainability highlights the importance of building structures and systems that endure.

Modern Application: Leaders can ensure long-term impact by:

- **Investing in People**: Develop team members' skills and leadership potential.
- **Documenting Innovations**: Create processes and frameworks that institutionalize successful practices.
- **Planning for Succession**: Prepare the next generation of leaders to carry the mission forward.

Practical Example: At *Health Empower*, leaders might create mentorship programs to develop future leaders, ensuring that innovation and adaptability remain core values of the organization.

7. Lessons For Modern Leaders

Key takeaways from Jesus' approach to innovation and adaptability include:

1. **Challenge the Status Quo Thoughtfully**: Innovation requires questioning traditions while respecting their value.
2. **Adapt to the Context**: Tailor strategies to meet the needs of different stakeholders and situations.
3. **Foster a Creative Culture**: Encourage experimentation and recognize innovative contributions.
4. **Maintain Consistency in Values**: Align new initiatives with the organization's mission and principles.
5. **Plan for Long-Term Impact**: Build systems and invest in people to sustain innovation over time.

Innovating With Purpose

Innovation and adaptability are essential for leaders navigating complex and rapidly changing environments. Jesus' example in the Gospel of Mark demonstrates that true innovation is not about chasing trends but about aligning new approaches with a clear mission and enduring values.

For leaders in mission-driven organizations like *Health Empower*, embracing these principles can drive meaningful change while building trust and resilience. By challenging the status quo, adapting to evolving circumstances, and fostering a culture of creativity, leaders can ensure their organization remains dynamic, impactful, and future-ready.

CHAPTER 9: CRISIS MANAGEMENT

◆ ◆ ◆

L eadership is most profoundly tested in moments of crisis. The Gospel of Mark provides powerful examples of Jesus navigating crises with clarity, composure, and compassion. Whether calming a storm, healing the sick, or addressing pressing challenges, Jesus demonstrates that effective crisis management requires a balance of action, trust, and steadfastness. In this chapter, we explore how Jesus managed crises, the principles He applied, and how modern leaders can leverage these lessons to navigate uncertainty and adversity.

1. Maintaining Composure Amid Chaos

Jesus Calms the Storm

In Mark 4:35-41, Jesus and His disciples are caught in a violent storm. As the boat fills with water, the disciples panic, exclaiming, "Teacher, don't you care if we drown?" Jesus, however, remains calm, rebukes the wind, and says to the waves, "Quiet! Be still!" His composed response not only resolves the immediate crisis but also strengthens the disciples' faith.

The Importance of Composure

Composure is contagious. In moments of crisis, a leader's demeanor can either escalate fear or inspire confidence. Jesus' ability to remain calm under pressure reassures His followers and allows Him to address the situation effectively.

Modern Application: Leaders must maintain composure during crises to inspire confidence and guide their teams. Strategies include:

- **Pause and Assess**: Take a moment to gather information and evaluate the situation before acting.
- **Model Confidence**: Demonstrate belief in the team's ability to overcome the challenge.
- **Stay Present**: Focus on immediate solutions rather than becoming overwhelmed by worst-case scenarios.

Practical Example: If a critical system fails at *Health Empower*, the leader might calmly convene the team, assess the issue, and outline a clear plan for resolution, ensuring panic does not disrupt problem-solving efforts.

2. Leading With Action And Decisiveness

Jesus' Response to the Hemorrhaging Woman

In Mark 5:25-34, while on His way to heal Jairus' daughter, Jesus is interrupted by a woman who touches His cloak in faith, seeking healing for her long-term illness. Despite the urgency of His original mission, Jesus stops, addresses the woman, and affirms her faith. This decisive action not only resolves her crisis but also reinforces His commitment to individual care.

The Role of Decisiveness

In crises, delayed action can exacerbate problems. Jesus

demonstrates the importance of taking timely, focused steps while balancing competing priorities.

Modern Application: Leaders can exhibit decisiveness in crises by:

- **Prioritizing Actions**: Identify the most critical issues and address them first.
- **Making Informed Decisions**: Gather key facts quickly and involve the right stakeholders.
- **Communicating Clearly**: Provide transparent updates on what is being done and why.

Practical Example: If a data breach occurs at *Health Empower*, the leadership team might immediately prioritize securing systems, notifying affected users, and coordinating a response with cybersecurity experts.

3. Balancing Urgency With Long-Term Vision

Jesus and Jairus' Daughter

In Mark 5:35-43, after the interruption with the hemorrhaging woman, Jesus continues to Jairus' home, only to find that the girl has died. Despite the grief and doubt surrounding Him, Jesus says, "Don't be afraid; just believe." He proceeds to raise the girl, demonstrating that even in dire circumstances, faith and focus can yield extraordinary results.

The Challenge of Balancing Immediate and Long-Term Needs

Crises often create pressure to focus solely on the immediate problem, but Jesus models the importance of addressing the moment without losing sight of the bigger picture.

Modern Application: Leaders must balance urgency with a commitment to the organization's long-term goals. Strategies include:

- **Focusing on Mission**: Ensure short-term actions align with the organization's overarching purpose.
- **Building Resilience**: Use the crisis as an opportunity to strengthen systems and prepare for future challenges.
- **Celebrating Wins**: Recognize milestones achieved during the crisis to maintain morale.

Practical Example: During a financial shortfall, *Health Empower* leaders might prioritize retaining core functionalities of their platform while exploring partnerships or grants to secure long-term sustainability.

4. Communicating Effectively During Crisis

Jesus' Use of Reassurance

Throughout Mark, Jesus reassures His followers during crises, calming their fears and refocusing their attention on solutions. For example, after calming the storm, He asks, "Why are you so afraid? Do you still have no faith?" (Mark 4:40). This question encourages reflection and trust, reinforcing His role as a dependable leader.

The Importance of Transparent Communication

In crises, uncertainty can lead to anxiety and confusion. Jesus' clear and compassionate communication ensures His followers remain informed and aligned.

Modern Application: Leaders must prioritize communication during crises to keep stakeholders engaged and reassured. Strategies include:

- **Regular Updates**: Provide frequent and accurate information to prevent speculation.
- **Empathy and Clarity**: Acknowledge challenges while offering actionable steps.
- **Two-Way Dialogue**: Create channels for feedback and

questions to ensure everyone feels heard.

Practical Example: If *Health Empower* faces user concerns about system outages, leaders could send regular status updates via email and in-app notifications, clearly outlining the steps being taken to resolve the issue.

5. Leveraging Team Strengths

Jesus Sends Out the Disciples

In Mark 6:7-13, Jesus delegates authority to His disciples, sending them out to preach, heal, and drive out demons. This delegation not only expands His mission but also empowers His team to act confidently in challenging situations.

Empowering Teams in Crisis

Crises often require collective effort. Jesus' approach highlights the importance of leveraging team strengths and fostering collaboration.

Modern Application: Leaders can empower their teams during crises by:

- **Delegating Responsibilities**: Assign roles based on expertise and capacity.
- **Encouraging Collaboration**: Foster teamwork to generate creative solutions.
- **Recognizing Contributions**: Celebrate team efforts to build morale and cohesion.

Practical Example: During a public relations crisis, *Health Empower* leaders might involve marketing, technical, and legal teams in crafting a unified response, ensuring every perspective is represented.

6. Turning Crises Into Opportunities

Jesus' Miracles as Transformative Moments

Many of Jesus' miracles in Mark arise from crises. Whether healing the sick, feeding the hungry, or calming storms, Jesus transforms challenges into opportunities to deepen faith and advance His mission.

Reframing Crisis as Growth

Jesus' actions demonstrate that crises can be transformative, offering opportunities for learning, growth, and innovation.

Modern Application: Leaders can use crises as catalysts for positive change by:

- **Identifying Lessons**: Analyze what went wrong and implement systemic improvements.
- **Strengthening Relationships**: Use the crisis to build trust with stakeholders through transparent and effective responses.
- **Innovating Solutions**: Develop new processes or products that address vulnerabilities revealed by the crisis.

Practical Example: If *Health Empower* faces a cybersecurity breach, leaders might enhance security measures and use the incident as an opportunity to educate users about data protection.

7. Lessons For Modern Leaders

From Jesus' handling of crises in the Gospel of Mark, leaders can draw several key lessons:

1. **Stay Composed**: A calm presence inspires confidence and enables effective decision-making.
2. **Act Decisively**: Address critical issues promptly while considering long-term implications.
3. **Communicate Transparently**: Keep stakeholders

informed with clear and empathetic messaging.

4. **Leverage Team Strengths**: Empower the team to collaborate and contribute solutions.

5. **Turn Challenges into Growth**: Use crises as opportunities to innovate and improve.

Leading Through Crisis With Faith And Focus

Crises are inevitable, but they also present leaders with opportunities to demonstrate resilience, adaptability, and commitment to their mission. Jesus' approach in the Gospel of Mark shows that effective crisis management requires not only decisive action but also compassion, communication, and a long-term perspective.

For leaders in organizations like *Health Empower*, these principles provide a framework for navigating uncertainty, addressing challenges with confidence, and emerging stronger on the other side. By embracing crises as opportunities for growth and transformation, leaders can inspire trust, build resilience, and drive meaningful impact.

CHAPTER 10: THE ROLE OF FAITH IN LEADERSHIP

◆ ◆ ◆

L eadership often involves navigating uncertainty, making difficult decisions, and inspiring others toward a vision. Faith, whether spiritual or grounded in a deeply held set of values, provides a foundation that can guide leaders through these challenges. In the Gospel of Mark, Jesus demonstrates the profound role of faith in leadership—faith in God, in the mission, and in the capacity of others to rise to their potential. This chapter explores how faith serves as an anchor for effective leadership, offering lessons for navigating crises, fostering resilience, and inspiring trust.

---

1. Faith as the Foundation of Leadership

Jesus' Faith in God's Mission

Throughout Mark, Jesus consistently demonstrates faith in

God's plan, even in the face of opposition and uncertainty. In Mark 1:35, Jesus retreats to pray in solitude, seeking strength and clarity. This reliance on God anchors His decisions and actions, ensuring alignment with His mission.

The Importance of a Higher Purpose

Faith in a higher purpose allows leaders to rise above immediate challenges and maintain focus on long-term goals. Jesus' unwavering trust in God's will, exemplified in Mark 14:36 ("Not what I will, but what You will"), reflects a deep commitment to serving a mission greater than Himself.

Application for Modern Leaders:

- Identify the core purpose or vision that drives your leadership.
- Foster faith in that purpose, using it as a compass in times of uncertainty.
- Develop a practice of reflection or prayer to align actions with values and goals.

---

2. Faith as a Source of Resilience

Faith in the Face of Crisis

In Mark 4:35-41, Jesus calms a storm while His disciples panic. His rebuke—"Why are you so afraid? Do you still have no faith?"—highlights the connection between faith and resilience. Jesus models calm and decisive leadership rooted in trust, even amidst chaos.

Overcoming Fear with Faith

Fear can paralyze leaders, but faith empowers them to act with confidence and clarity. Jesus' example shows that resilience stems from a belief in the mission and the resources available to fulfill it, whether spiritual or practical.

Application for Modern Leaders:

- Cultivate a mindset of faith to counteract fear and doubt during crises.
- Encourage your team to trust in their collective ability to overcome challenges.
- Reflect on past successes as evidence of the mission's viability and strength.

---

3. Faith as a Catalyst for Action

Faith and Boldness

In Mark 2:1-12, the friends of a paralyzed man demonstrate faith by lowering him through a roof to reach Jesus. Their boldness inspires Jesus to heal the man, saying, "Your sins are forgiven." This moment underscores how faith fuels action, even in the face of obstacles.

Leadership Requires Bold Decisions

Faith empowers leaders to take bold, calculated risks. It allows them to act decisively, trusting in their preparation, team, and vision to achieve success.

Application for Modern Leaders:

- Translate faith into bold, mission-aligned actions that inspire your team.

- Take calculated risks when opportunities align with your purpose and values.
- Lead with conviction, encouraging others to embrace challenges with confidence.

---

4. Faith in Others

Jesus' Faith in His Disciples

Despite their imperfections, Jesus invests deeply in His disciples, entrusting them with significant responsibilities. In Mark 6:7-13, He sends them out to preach and heal, demonstrating faith in their ability to carry out His mission. Even when they falter, as in Mark 9:14-29, Jesus uses the opportunity to teach and build their faith.

Building Trust and Empowering Teams

Faith in others is essential for effective delegation and team-building. By believing in their potential and offering support, leaders empower their teams to grow and succeed.

Application for Modern Leaders:

- Invest in your team, recognizing their potential for growth and leadership.
- Provide opportunities for others to take ownership of tasks and responsibilities.
- Offer encouragement and constructive feedback to build confidence and trust.

---

5. Faith as a Guide in Ethical Leadership

Jesus' Integrity in Leadership

Jesus consistently prioritizes ethical principles over expediency. In Mark 12:13-17, He responds to a politically charged question about taxes with wisdom and integrity, saying, "Give back to Caesar what is Caesar's and to God what is God's." This response reflects faith in the power of truth and justice to guide decision-making.

Staying True to Values

Faith in a higher moral standard helps leaders navigate ethical dilemmas. It provides the courage to stand firm in the face of pressure or temptation to compromise.

Application for Modern Leaders:

- Anchor decisions in ethical principles, even when they conflict with short-term gains.
- Communicate the importance of integrity to your team, fostering a culture of accountability.
- Trust that staying true to your values will yield long-term success and respect.

---

6. Faith in the Unseen

The Paradox of Faith

Faith often involves believing in outcomes that are not yet visible. In Mark 11:22-24, Jesus teaches His disciples to have faith in God, saying, "Whatever you ask for in prayer, believe that you have received it, and it will be yours." This principle underscores the power of belief to inspire action and perseverance.

Vision Beyond Immediate Results

Leaders must often work toward goals that are not immediately achievable. Faith in the vision allows them to persevere, even when progress is slow or obstacles arise.

Application for Modern Leaders:

- Cultivate a long-term perspective, trusting in the process even when results are not immediate.
- Inspire others by sharing a vision of what is possible and encouraging them to work toward it.
- Maintain optimism and perseverance, trusting that efforts will bear fruit in time.

---

7. The Role of Faith in Inspiring Others

Jesus' Influence Through Faith

Jesus' faith in God and His mission inspired those around Him, drawing crowds and transforming lives. His confidence and conviction attracted followers and encouraged them to embrace a higher calling.

Faith as a Source of Influence

Leaders who demonstrate genuine faith in their mission and team inspire trust, loyalty, and enthusiasm. Their belief becomes contagious, motivating others to rise to the challenge.

Application for Modern Leaders:

- Communicate your faith in the mission and your team

through words and actions.
- Lead with authenticity, allowing your conviction to inspire confidence in others.
- Celebrate successes and milestones to reinforce the collective belief in the vision.

Conclusion

Faith is the cornerstone of transformative leadership. As demonstrated by Jesus in the Gospel of Mark, faith empowers leaders to navigate uncertainty, inspire others, and stay true to their mission. It provides resilience in crises, courage in decision-making, and a foundation for ethical and impactful leadership. For modern leaders, faith—whether spiritual or rooted in deeply held values—can serve as a guiding force, enabling them to lead with conviction, integrity, and hope. By cultivating faith in their mission, their team, and the unseen possibilities of the future, leaders can create lasting impact and inspire others to join them on the journey toward meaningful change.

CHAPTER 11: REDEFINING SUCCESS AND FAILURE

◆ ◆ ◆

In leadership, success is often measured by tangible outcomes such as profits, growth metrics, or societal recognition. However, the Gospel of Mark challenges conventional definitions of success and failure. Jesus' ministry, from a worldly perspective, included moments that appeared to be failures: rejection, betrayal, and ultimately crucifixion. Yet these moments were integral to His ultimate mission and triumph. This chapter explores how leaders can redefine success and failure, focusing on long-term impact, purpose-driven goals, and the transformative power of setbacks.

---

1. Jesus' Counter-Cultural Definition of Success

Worldly Success vs. Kingdom Success

In Mark 8:34-37, Jesus teaches His disciples about the cost of following Him: "Whoever wants to save their life will lose it, but whoever loses their life for me and for the gospel will save it." This paradoxical statement redefines success as surrendering personal ambitions to pursue a higher purpose.

Lessons for Leaders

Success is not merely achieving visible outcomes but aligning actions with core values and mission. Jesus' rejection of societal metrics—wealth, power, and status—underscores the importance of focusing on eternal and transformative goals.

Application for Modern Leaders:

- Define success in terms of mission fulfillment rather than short-term wins.
- Evaluate decisions based on their alignment with organizational values and long-term objectives.
- Resist the temptation to prioritize optics over substance, choosing meaningful impact over immediate recognition.

---

2. Learning from Apparent Failures

The Cross as a Symbol of Triumph

In Mark 15:33-39, Jesus' crucifixion appears to be the ultimate failure. Yet, from a spiritual perspective, it represents the culmination of His mission. His death and resurrection highlight that apparent defeat can lead to ultimate victory when viewed through the lens of purpose.

Failure as a Catalyst for Growth

Jesus' endurance through trials demonstrates how setbacks can serve a greater purpose. For leaders, failures often provide opportunities to refine strategies, strengthen character, and build resilience.

Application for Modern Leaders:

- Reframe failures as learning experiences that contribute to growth and innovation.
- Analyze setbacks to identify lessons and systemic improvements.
- Communicate the value of perseverance to your team, emphasizing that setbacks are part of the journey toward meaningful success.

---

3. The Role of Integrity in Defining Success

Jesus' Refusal to Compromise

In Mark 12:13-17, Jesus is asked whether it is lawful to pay taxes to Caesar—a question designed to trap Him. His response, "Give back to Caesar what is Caesar's and to God what is God's," reflects His ability to navigate challenges without compromising His integrity or mission.

Prioritizing Principles Over Results

Jesus' example shows that true success is grounded in integrity, even when it comes at a cost. Leaders who prioritize ethics over expediency build trust and create lasting impact.

Application for Modern Leaders:

- Define success by how closely decisions align with ethical principles, even if it requires sacrificing short-term gains.

- Foster a culture of integrity within your organization, where values guide actions.
- Measure success not only by outcomes but also by the process and adherence to core principles.

---

4. Overcoming Societal Expectations

Rejection in His Hometown

In Mark 6:1-6, Jesus is rejected in Nazareth, where people question His authority and dismiss Him as merely "the carpenter." This moment underscores how societal expectations can obscure true potential and purpose.

Staying Mission-Focused

Despite rejection, Jesus continues His work, demonstrating that leaders must remain committed to their vision even when others fail to recognize its value.

Application for Modern Leaders:

- Stay focused on long-term goals, even when facing skepticism or rejection.
- Recognize that societal expectations do not define your success; your alignment with purpose does.
- Encourage your team to persevere in the face of external criticism, reinforcing the value of staying true to the mission.

---

5. Success Through Empowering Others

Delegation and Multiplication

In Mark 6:7-13, Jesus sends out the twelve disciples to preach and heal. By empowering His followers, He extends the reach of His mission, demonstrating that true success involves equipping others to carry forward the vision.

The Ripple Effect

Jesus' leadership shows that success is not just about individual achievements but about the legacy left through others. Leaders who invest in their teams create a multiplier effect that extends their impact far beyond their tenure.

Application for Modern Leaders:

- Measure success by the growth and development of those you lead.
- Delegate responsibilities and empower your team to contribute to the mission.
- Focus on building a legacy of shared success, ensuring the mission continues to thrive after your departure.

---

6. Balancing Immediate Outcomes with Eternal Goals

The Feeding of the Five Thousand

In Mark 6:30-44, Jesus feeds a multitude with limited resources, meeting an immediate need while teaching about God's provision. This balance of addressing present concerns while pointing to eternal truths highlights the importance of multi-layered success.

Sustaining Vision Through Practical Wins

While ultimate goals often take time, achieving small wins along the way builds momentum and reinforces the mission's viability. Leaders can use these milestones to maintain focus and inspire others.

Application for Modern Leaders:

- Break down long-term goals into achievable steps to demonstrate progress.
- Celebrate small victories as evidence of the mission's success and sustainability.
- Maintain a vision of ultimate goals, ensuring that immediate actions contribute to broader objectives.

---

7. Success as Transformation, Not Transaction

Healing and Forgiveness

In Mark 2:1-12, Jesus heals a paralyzed man but first forgives his sins, prioritizing spiritual restoration over physical healing. This moment underscores that success is not merely transactional but transformative, addressing deeper needs.

Transformative Leadership

Leaders succeed when they create lasting change in people, systems, or organizations. Focusing on transformation rather than transactional outcomes leads to deeper, more meaningful impact.

Application for Modern Leaders:

- Focus on creating systems and cultures that foster long-term transformation.
- Evaluate success by the depth and sustainability of your impact, not just surface-level metrics.
- Prioritize people over processes, ensuring that individual growth is part of the mission.

Conclusion

Redefining success and failure challenges leaders to look beyond conventional metrics and embrace a purpose-driven perspective. Jesus' example in the Gospel of Mark demonstrates that true success is not about immediate results but about alignment with values, resilience through setbacks, and the legacy of transformation left behind. For modern leaders, this redefinition offers a path to meaningful impact, where failures become stepping stones and success is measured by faithfulness to the mission. By embracing this approach, leaders can inspire others, build lasting change, and leave a legacy that transcends their personal achievements.

CHAPTER 12:
THE COST OF
LEADERSHIP

◆ ◆ ◆

L
eadership is often portrayed as a position of power, influence, and success. Yet, true leadership comes with significant costs—personal, emotional, and sometimes physical. In the Gospel of Mark, Jesus exemplifies leadership that embraces sacrifice for the sake of others, highlighting the price leaders must pay to remain faithful to their mission. This chapter explores the costs of leadership, the challenges leaders face in fulfilling their responsibilities, and the principles Jesus modeled for navigating these sacrifices with courage and grace.

---

1. Sacrificing Comfort for Mission

Jesus' Relentless Commitment

Throughout Mark, Jesus prioritizes His mission over personal comfort. In Mark 1:35-39, He rises early to pray in solitude, even after an exhausting day of healing and teaching. When His disciples suggest staying in one place to build on His popularity, Jesus insists on moving to other villages to continue preaching, reflecting a commitment to purpose over convenience.

The Leader's Sacrifice of Comfort

Effective leaders often forgo personal ease to serve their team and mission. Whether working long hours, making difficult decisions, or facing external criticism, leadership requires a willingness to prioritize the greater good over personal desires.

Application for Modern Leaders:

- Accept that leadership often involves inconvenience and sacrifice.
- Develop routines, like prayer or reflection, to stay focused and re-energized amid demanding responsibilities.
- Prioritize mission-driven decisions over personal comfort or popularity.

---

2. Bearing the Weight of Responsibility

Jesus' Leadership Burden

In Mark 6:30-44, Jesus feeds five thousand people after His disciples suggest sending them away. Despite seeking rest after intense ministry, Jesus takes on the responsibility of addressing their need, demonstrating compassion and initiative. His burden is not just logistical but emotional, as He continually responds to the demands of those around Him.

The Emotional Cost of Leadership

Leaders often bear the weight of their team's challenges, expectations, and failures. This responsibility can lead to stress, self-doubt, and emotional exhaustion if not managed effectively.

Application for Modern Leaders:

- Acknowledge the emotional toll of leadership and seek support from trusted advisors or mentors.
- Establish boundaries to balance the needs of the team with personal well-being.
- Cultivate resilience through self-care, reflection, and a reliance on faith or inner values.

---

3. Facing Rejection and Criticism

Jesus' Rejection

In Mark 6:1-6, Jesus is rejected in His hometown, where people question His authority and dismiss Him as merely "the carpenter." Despite His wisdom and miracles, He faces skepticism and disbelief, reflecting the reality that even the most capable leaders encounter resistance.

The Leader's Experience with Criticism

Criticism and rejection are inevitable for leaders, especially when making difficult or unpopular decisions. The challenge lies in maintaining focus and confidence despite external opposition.

Application for Modern Leaders:

- Separate constructive feedback from baseless criticism,

using the former to improve and disregarding the latter.

- Remain mission-focused, trusting in the vision even when others doubt it.
- Draw strength from a supportive community or faith to persevere through rejection.

4. Enduring Betrayal and Isolation

Jesus' Betrayal

In Mark 14:43-50, Judas betrays Jesus with a kiss, and the disciples flee during His arrest, leaving Him isolated in His moment of greatest need. Despite this, Jesus remains steadfast, focusing on His mission rather than the personal pain of abandonment.

Betrayal in Leadership

Leaders often face betrayal from trusted individuals, whether through broken trust, criticism, or lack of support. Such moments can lead to isolation and disillusionment if not navigated with resilience and grace.

Application for Modern Leaders:

- Recognize betrayal as a painful but often unavoidable aspect of leadership.
- Respond with grace, focusing on the mission rather than personal grievances.
- Build a diverse network of trusted allies to reduce the risk of complete isolation.

5. The Cost of Ethical Leadership

Jesus' Integrity

In Mark 12:13-17, Jesus refuses to be trapped by the Pharisees' question about paying taxes. His response—"Give back to Caesar what is Caesar's and to God what is God's"—balances wisdom and integrity, avoiding compromise while addressing the issue.

The Challenge of Staying Ethical

Ethical leadership often comes at a cost, as leaders face pressure to compromise values for convenience, profit, or political gain. Maintaining integrity may result in lost opportunities, strained relationships, or even personal danger.

Application for Modern Leaders:

- Prioritize integrity over expediency, even when it requires personal or professional sacrifice.
- Communicate ethical principles clearly to your team, fostering a culture of accountability.
- Trust that long-term respect and trustworthiness outweigh short-term gains from compromise.

---

6. Sacrificing Personal Glory for Team Success

Jesus' Delegation

In Mark 6:7-13, Jesus sends His disciples to preach and heal, giving them authority to act in His name. By empowering others, Jesus sacrifices the opportunity to do everything Himself, instead focusing on multiplying His impact through His team.

The Leader's Sacrifice of Credit

True leadership often involves allowing others to take credit for success, prioritizing team growth and mission impact over personal recognition. This selflessness builds trust and fosters collaboration.

Application for Modern Leaders:

- Delegate responsibilities to empower team members, even if it means stepping out of the spotlight.
- Celebrate team successes publicly, giving credit to those who contribute.
- Focus on the mission's success rather than personal accolades.

---

7. Paying the Ultimate Price

Jesus' Sacrificial Death

In Mark 15:33-39, Jesus pays the ultimate price for His mission, laying down His life to fulfill God's plan. His sacrifice reflects the highest cost of leadership: giving everything for the sake of others.

The Call to Sacrificial Leadership

While few leaders face such extreme demands, true leadership often involves putting the mission and others' needs above personal gain. Sacrificial leadership inspires loyalty, trust, and lasting impact.

Application for Modern Leaders:

- Embrace sacrifice as a part of leadership, whether it involves time, resources, or personal ambition.
- Lead with humility, prioritizing the well-being and success of those you serve.
- Inspire your team by modeling selflessness and a commitment to the greater good.

8. Finding Strength Amid the Costs

Jesus' Source of Strength

Throughout Mark, Jesus draws strength from His relationship with God, frequently retreating to pray (Mark 1:35, Mark 6:46). His reliance on prayer and solitude enables Him to persevere through the demands of leadership.

Sustaining Leadership Through Faith

Faith or deeply held values can provide leaders with the strength to endure the costs of leadership. By staying connected to a higher purpose, leaders can navigate challenges with resilience and hope.

Application for Modern Leaders:

- Develop a practice of reflection or prayer to stay grounded in your mission.
- Surround yourself with a supportive community or trusted advisors.
- Revisit your purpose regularly, using it as motivation to persevere through challenges.

Conclusion

Leadership is a privilege, but it comes with significant costs. From sacrificing comfort and enduring criticism to facing betrayal and maintaining integrity, leaders must navigate challenges with courage and selflessness. Jesus' example in the Gospel of Mark demonstrates that these costs are not burdens but opportunities to serve others and fulfill a higher purpose. By embracing the sacrifices of leadership, modern leaders can inspire trust, foster meaningful change, and leave a legacy of integrity and impact. Ultimately, the cost of leadership is a reflection of its value—an investment in a mission greater than oneself.

CHAPTER 13: LEGACY AND SUCCESSION PLANNING

◆ ◆ ◆

The measure of a leader is not just the impact they make during their lifetime but the legacy they leave behind. In the Gospel of Mark, Jesus exemplifies intentional legacy-building and succession planning. By preparing His disciples to carry on His mission after His departure, Jesus ensures the continuation and expansion of His work. This chapter explores the principles of legacy and succession planning as modeled by Jesus, offering insights for modern leaders seeking to build enduring impact within their organizations.

1. The Vision For Legacy

Jesus' Long-Term Focus

Throughout His ministry, Jesus emphasizes the eternal nature of His mission. In Mark 16:15-20, He commissions His disciples to "go into all the world and preach the gospel to all creation." This clear articulation of purpose ensures His vision transcends His earthly ministry.

Core Elements of a Lasting Legacy

- **Mission-Driven Leadership**: A legacy is rooted in a leader's commitment to a mission greater than themselves.
- **Empowered Successors**: A leader's impact continues when others are equipped to sustain and grow the vision.
- **Sustainable Systems**: Establishing frameworks and practices ensures continuity beyond the leader's tenure.

Modern Application: For leaders in mission-driven organizations like *Health Empower*, creating a legacy means building a purpose-driven culture that persists even as leadership changes. This involves:

- Defining a compelling mission and vision.
- Communicating the organization's core values consistently.
- Empowering team members to take ownership of the mission.

2. Identifying And Developing Successors

Jesus' Selection of Disciples

In Mark 3:13-19, Jesus calls His disciples, investing time and energy in a small group who will carry on His mission. He chooses individuals with diverse backgrounds and strengths, focusing on their potential rather than their current capabilities.

Personal Investment in Development

Jesus spends significant time teaching, mentoring, and challenging His disciples. For example, in Mark 4:10-12, He provides deeper explanations of His parables, equipping them with the knowledge and understanding needed to lead.

Modern Application: Leaders can identify and develop

successors by:

- **Assessing Potential**: Look for individuals who demonstrate alignment with organizational values, a willingness to learn, and the ability to inspire others.
- **Providing Mentorship**: Offer guidance, feedback, and opportunities for growth.
- **Encouraging Initiative**: Allow emerging leaders to take on responsibility and make decisions, fostering confidence and experience.

Practical Example: At *Health Empower*, leaders might identify high-potential employees and involve them in strategic projects or leadership training programs, ensuring they are prepared to take on greater responsibilities.

3. Gradual Transition Of Responsibility

Jesus' Delegation and Empowerment

In Mark 6:7-13, Jesus sends out His disciples two by two, giving them authority to preach, heal, and drive out demons. This delegation allows the disciples to practice leadership under His guidance, building their confidence and competence.

Phased Succession

Jesus introduces leadership responsibilities gradually, balancing empowerment with support. By the time He commissions them in Mark 16:15-20, the disciples are ready to lead independently.

Modern Application: Effective succession planning involves a gradual transfer of responsibilities to ensure continuity. Strategies include:

- **Start Small**: Assign manageable leadership tasks to

emerging leaders and provide feedback.

- **Increase Complexity**: Gradually expand their responsibilities to prepare them for larger roles.
- **Provide Oversight**: Remain available as a mentor and resource during the transition.

Practical Example: A leader at *Health Empower* might start by delegating team management to a promising employee, eventually involving them in high-stakes decisions to prepare them for executive roles.

4. Communicating The Vision

Jesus' Clarity in Commissioning

Jesus articulates His vision clearly to His disciples, ensuring they understand their role in continuing His mission. In Mark 16:15, He says, "Go into all the world and preach the gospel to all creation," providing a concise yet profound directive.

Reinforcement Through Repetition

Throughout Mark, Jesus reiterates His mission and values, embedding them in His disciples' minds. This repetition ensures alignment and commitment.

Modern Application: Leaders must communicate their vision effectively to ensure continuity. Strategies include:

- **Articulating the Vision**: Clearly define the organization's mission and goals.
- **Reinforcing Core Values**: Regularly emphasize the principles that guide decision-making.
- **Engaging Stakeholders**: Involve team members in discussions about the organization's future to foster ownership and alignment.

Practical Example: At *Health Empower*, leaders might hold regular town halls to discuss the company's mission, celebrate progress, and reaffirm the vision, ensuring all team members are aligned.

5. Building Sustainable Systems

Jesus' Establishment of Practices

Jesus ensures sustainability by instilling practices such as prayer, teaching, and service. These habits form the foundation of the disciples' leadership after His departure.

The Importance of Systems

By teaching His disciples to rely on principles rather than His physical presence, Jesus ensures His mission continues seamlessly. For example, He emphasizes prayer as a source of strength and guidance (Mark 1:35).

Modern Application: Sustainability in leadership involves creating systems and structures that outlast individual leaders. Strategies include:

- **Standardizing Processes**: Develop frameworks and guidelines that ensure consistency.
- **Documenting Knowledge**: Create accessible resources to preserve institutional knowledge.
- **Fostering Autonomy**: Encourage teams to operate independently while maintaining alignment with the mission.

Practical Example: *Health Empower* might implement documented workflows, knowledge-sharing platforms, and decision-making frameworks to ensure operational continuity during leadership transitions.

6. Overcoming Resistance To Succession

Challenges in Transition

Transitions often face resistance, as individuals may fear change or question the readiness of successors. Jesus addresses such challenges by maintaining transparency and fostering trust. For example, in Mark 8:31-33, He prepares His disciples for His eventual departure, even as they struggle to accept it.

Earning Trust

Jesus builds trust through consistent leadership and personal investment in His disciples, ensuring they believe in His vision and their role in it.

Modern Application: Leaders can navigate resistance to succession by:

- **Communicating Early**: Discuss succession plans openly to build confidence.
- **Demonstrating Competence**: Showcase the readiness of successors through their achievements.
- **Reinforcing Stability**: Emphasize continuity in mission and values during transitions.

Practical Example: If a leadership change is planned at *Health Empower*, current leaders might introduce successors gradually, highlighting their contributions and capabilities to build trust across the organization.

7. Measuring Success And Impact

Jesus' Legacy

The success of Jesus' succession planning is evident in the growth of His disciples' impact after His ascension. In Mark 16:20, the disciples "went out and preached everywhere, and the Lord worked with them and confirmed His word by the signs that accompanied it." This enduring impact reflects the effectiveness of His leadership and preparation.

Indicators of Success

- **Mission Continuity**: The organization remains aligned with its purpose after the transition.
- **Team Confidence**: Successors feel equipped and empowered to lead.
- **Long-Term Growth**: The mission continues to expand and adapt to future challenges.

Modern Application: Leaders can evaluate the success of succession planning by:

- Monitoring organizational performance during and after transitions.
- Soliciting feedback from stakeholders on the process and outcomes.
- Celebrating milestones that demonstrate the continuity and growth of the mission.

Leading Beyond Your Time

Jesus' leadership in the Gospel of Mark demonstrates that succession planning and legacy-building are essential components of effective leadership. By empowering His disciples, articulating a clear vision, and establishing sustainable practices, He ensures His mission continues to thrive.

For leaders in modern organizations like *Health Empower*, these principles offer a roadmap for creating a lasting legacy. By investing in people, communicating purpose, and preparing for transitions, leaders can ensure their impact endures, inspiring future generations to carry the mission forward with confidence and purpose.

Timeless Leadership Principles For Transformative Impact

Leadership is both an art and a responsibility. The Gospel of Mark offers a vivid portrait of Jesus as a leader who inspired, empowered, and transformed those around Him. His principles —rooted in clarity of mission, servant-hearted humility, and an unwavering commitment to truth—resonate deeply with the challenges and opportunities faced by modern leaders.

From casting a compelling vision to managing crises, from building trust to empowering others, Jesus' leadership transcends cultural and historical boundaries. He balanced decisiveness with empathy, innovation with consistency, and authority with service. His actions were not only effective but also deeply relational, reflecting a profound understanding of the human heart and its capacity for growth.

Key Takeaways For Modern Leaders

As we reflect on the leadership principles of Jesus as portrayed in Mark, several lessons emerge that are universally applicable:

1. **Clarity of Mission and Vision**: Define your purpose and let it guide every decision.
2. **Empowering Others**: Build a team that shares your mission and invest in their growth.
3. **Servant Leadership**: Lead by serving, prioritizing the needs of others over personal gain.
4. **Adaptability and Innovation**: Embrace change and think creatively while staying true to your core values.
5. **Crisis Management**: Remain calm, decisive, and focused on long-term goals during challenges.
6. **Succession Planning**: Prepare future leaders to carry

the mission forward with confidence and competence.

A Model For Purposeful Leadership

Jesus' leadership offers more than strategies for success; it provides a model for purposeful, transformative leadership that uplifts others and creates lasting impact. His example challenges leaders to lead with integrity, compassion, and a commitment to something greater than themselves.

Carrying The Lessons Forward

Whether you are leading a startup, a global organization, a small team, or even your family, the principles explored in this book provide a framework for impactful leadership. Like Jesus, you have the opportunity to inspire trust, guide others through challenges, and create a legacy that extends beyond your immediate influence.

Leadership is not about achieving greatness for yourself but about enabling greatness in others. By applying these timeless principles, you can lead with purpose, navigate complexity with grace, and leave an indelible mark on the lives of those you serve.

As you move forward in your leadership journey, may you embody these principles with courage and conviction, transforming not only your organization but also the world around you.

CASE STUDY: APPLYING LEADERSHIP PRINCIPLES TO A HEALTHCARE STARTUP

◆ ◆ ◆

Imagine a healthcare startup, HealthEmpower, with a mission to empower underserved communities by providing affordable, technology-driven solutions to manage chronic diseases. The company aims to offer mobile-first platforms for health tracking, virtual consultations, and community health education. However, it operates in a highly regulated, resource-constrained environment, where access to technology and healthcare infrastructure is limited.

This case study explores how the leadership principles modeled by Jesus in the Gospel of Mark can guide HealthEmpower's founder to navigate industry-specific challenges, such as regulatory compliance, integration with existing healthcare systems, and fostering trust in underserved communities. These principles provide a framework for ethical and innovative leadership that aligns with the company's mission while addressing real-world obstacles.

1. Clarifying Mission and Vision

Challenge

Operating in underserved communities requires a clear, compelling mission that aligns all stakeholders. HealthEmpower's mission is "to democratize healthcare by providing accessible, affordable, and culturally sensitive solutions to manage chronic diseases."

Application of Leadership Principles

Like Jesus' clarity in proclaiming the Kingdom of God (Mark 1:15), the founder must articulate this mission consistently to inspire internal teams and external partners.

Actions:

- Develop a mission-driven culture where every decision aligns with the company's purpose.
- Communicate the mission through outreach campaigns targeting patients, providers, and community leaders.
- Use patient stories to demonstrate how the platform improves lives, fostering emotional connection and trust.

2. Navigating Regulatory Frameworks

Challenge

HealthEmpower must comply with stringent regulations such as HIPAA for data privacy and medical device approval processes for diagnostics tools.

Application of Leadership Principles

Jesus' response to the Pharisees' attempts to trap Him (Mark 12:13-17) shows the importance of wisdom and integrity when navigating complex systems. Similarly, the founder must embrace compliance as a non-negotiable aspect of ethical leadership.

Actions:

- Partner with legal and regulatory experts to ensure the platform meets all requirements.
- Implement robust data security measures, including encryption and regular audits, to protect patient information.
- Train employees on regulatory compliance to foster a culture of accountability.

Example: HealthEmpower collaborates with a regulatory consultancy to streamline the FDA approval process for its AI-driven diagnostic tool.

---

3. Integrating Technology into Underserved Communities

Challenge

Limited internet connectivity, low health literacy, and cultural barriers can hinder adoption of HealthEmpower's platform in underserved areas.

Application of Leadership Principles

Jesus' use of parables (Mark 4:1-20) demonstrates how to communicate complex ideas in a relatable way. Similarly, HealthEmpower must adapt its technology and messaging to meet users where they are.

Actions:

- Design a mobile-first platform optimized for low-bandwidth environments, including offline functionality.
- Translate content into multiple languages and use culturally sensitive visuals.
- Engage local leaders and health workers to act as ambassadors, building trust and encouraging adoption.

Example: HealthEmpower deploys its app in rural areas by partnering with community health clinics, offering in-person workshops to teach users how to leverage its features.

---

4. Collaborating with Existing Healthcare Systems

Challenge

HealthEmpower needs to integrate seamlessly with hospitals, insurance providers, and pharmacies to ensure continuity of care for patients.

Application of Leadership Principles

Jesus' ability to collaborate with diverse groups, including disciples and broader audiences, emphasizes the value of partnerships. In Mark 6:7-13, He sends out disciples to extend His mission—a lesson in multiplying impact through collaboration.

Actions:

- Use FHIR standards to integrate the platform with electronic health record (EHR) systems.
- Build APIs to facilitate data exchange with pharmacies and labs.
- Partner with hospitals to ensure the platform complements existing workflows.

Example: HealthEmpower pilots its platform with a regional hospital network, enabling seamless virtual consultations integrated with patients' medical records.

---

5. Funding and Sustainability

Challenge

Balancing affordability for underserved populations with the need for financial sustainability is a critical challenge.

Application of Leadership Principles

In Mark 6:30-44, Jesus feeds five thousand people with limited resources, emphasizing creativity and resourcefulness. Similarly, HealthEmpower's founder must explore diverse funding models to achieve sustainability.

Actions:

- Secure government grants for rural health initiatives.
- Partner with impact investors focused on social good.

- Offer a tiered subscription model, with premium services subsidizing free access for low-income users.

Example: HealthEmpower secures a public-private partnership with a state government to expand telemedicine access in underserved regions.

---

6. Measuring Impact and Outcomes

Challenge

Demonstrating measurable outcomes is essential to gain stakeholder trust and drive adoption.

Application of Leadership Principles

Jesus often demonstrated tangible outcomes of His mission, such as healing the sick or feeding the hungry (Mark 5:25-34). Similarly, HealthEmpower must provide evidence of its effectiveness.

Actions:

- Use KPIs like reduced hospital readmissions, improved chronic disease management, and increased user engagement to track success.
- Publish real-world evidence studies to validate the platform's impact.
- Share patient testimonials to highlight the human stories behind the data.

Example: HealthEmpower's six-month pilot program shows a 30% improvement in medication adherence among diabetic patients in rural areas.

---

7. Addressing Workforce Challenges

Challenge

Underserved regions often face a shortage of qualified healthcare professionals, limiting the platform's reach.

Application of Leadership Principles

In Mark 6:7-13, Jesus empowers His disciples to take on leadership roles. HealthEmpower's founder must similarly invest in training local workers.

Actions:

- Partner with local educational institutions to train community health workers.
- Develop certification programs for telehealth facilitators.
- Leverage AI tools to augment healthcare providers' capabilities, reducing workload.

Example: HealthEmpower launches a community health worker program, training 100 individuals to deliver basic care and use the platform effectively.

---

8. Adapting to Policy Changes

Challenge

Dynamic healthcare policies, such as telemedicine reimbursement models, can disrupt operations or create new opportunities.

Application of Leadership Principles

Jesus' agility in responding to evolving circumstances, such as His strategic handling of political traps (Mark 12:13-17), highlights the need for adaptability.

Actions:

- Monitor policy developments and align the platform with government initiatives.
- Adjust pricing or business models to leverage new reimbursement policies.
- Advocate for telehealth-friendly policies through partnerships with industry associations.

Example: HealthEmpower adjusts its business model to benefit from new state subsidies for chronic disease management programs.

Conclusion

By addressing these challenges with the leadership principles modeled by Jesus, HealthEmpower's founder can create a scalable, impactful solution that transforms healthcare for underserved communities. The integration of ethical decision-making, innovation, and community engagement ensures that the startup not only navigates obstacles effectively but also fulfills its mission to empower individuals and improve lives. This case study demonstrates that purpose-driven leadership, rooted in resilience and adaptability, is the key to lasting success in the complex world of healthcare.

CASE STUDY: APPLYING JESUS' LEADERSHIP PRINCIPLES TO ETHICAL GOVERNANCE

◆ ◆ ◆

L eading a government agency at any level—local, state, or national—comes with immense responsibility and challenges, particularly in environments rife with corruption. A leader committed to serving the community and improving the quality of life must navigate systemic obstacles while maintaining integrity and focus on the mission. The leadership principles modeled by Jesus in the Gospel of Mark offer a powerful framework for ethical and effective governance. These principles can guide leaders in maintaining their moral compass, fostering change, and inspiring trust in their leadership without being tainted or subverted by the corrupt systems they aim to reform.

1. Clarifying Mission And Vision

Jesus' Principle

Jesus maintained unwavering clarity about His mission to proclaim the Kingdom of God (Mark 1:15). This focus guided all His decisions and actions, allowing Him to resist distractions and opposition.

Application to Government Leadership

A leader in a government agency must define and communicate a clear mission focused on community service, accountability, and improving quality of life. This clarity acts as a safeguard against corruption and aligns the agency's efforts with its purpose.

Action Steps:

- **Define the Agency's Mission**: For example, "To deliver transparent, efficient, and impactful public services that improve the lives of citizens."
- **Communicate the Vision**: Ensure the team understands the mission and its importance, reinforcing it regularly.
- **Set Accountability Standards**: Implement systems that measure success based on service impact and integrity.

2. Leading By Example

Jesus' Principle

Jesus consistently modeled the values He taught, embodying humility, compassion, and obedience to God's will (Mark 10:45).

His example inspired trust and commitment in His followers.

Application to Government Leadership

Leaders must exemplify ethical behavior and transparency, demonstrating a commitment to integrity even in challenging environments. By modeling the behavior they expect, they can inspire their teams and build credibility.

Action Steps:

- **Demonstrate Integrity**: Refuse bribes, favoritism, or unethical shortcuts, even at personal or professional cost.
- **Be Transparent**: Share decision-making processes openly to build trust with staff and the public.
- **Prioritize Service**: Focus on delivering tangible benefits to the community, emphasizing the importance of public service over personal gain.

3. Building And Empowering A Team

Jesus' Principle

Jesus selected a small, diverse group of disciples and invested deeply in their development (Mark 3:13-19). He empowered them with authority to continue His mission (Mark 6:7-13).

Application to Government Leadership

A leader must surround themselves with individuals who share their commitment to integrity and service, investing in their professional growth and creating a culture of accountability.

Action Steps:

- **Recruit Ethical Team Members**: Prioritize character and values over credentials when hiring or promoting.
- **Invest in Training**: Provide team members with training on

ethics, leadership, and public service excellence.

- **Empower Delegation**: Trust team members with responsibilities, ensuring they have the resources and support to succeed.

4. Handling Opposition And Conflict

Jesus' Principle

Jesus faced relentless opposition from religious leaders and skeptics, yet He responded with grace and truth, remaining focused on His mission (Mark 2:6-7, Mark 12:13-17).

Application to Government Leadership

In corrupt systems, leaders will face opposition from individuals or groups who resist change. Addressing such conflicts with wisdom and firmness is essential to advancing the mission without compromising integrity.

Action Steps:

- **Address Corruption Directly**: Establish clear anti-corruption policies and enforce them consistently.
- **Stay Composed Under Pressure**: Avoid emotional responses to criticism or resistance, focusing instead on long-term goals.
- **Engage Critics Constructively**: Respond to valid concerns with humility, using criticism as an opportunity for growth or improvement.

5. Innovation And Adaptability

Jesus' Principle

Jesus adapted His teaching methods to suit different audiences, using parables for the crowds and deeper explanations for His disciples (Mark 4:1-20, Mark 4:34).

Application to Government Leadership

Innovation and adaptability are critical for navigating systemic obstacles and introducing meaningful reform. Leaders must find creative solutions to long-standing issues without compromising their values.

Action Steps

- **Streamline Processes**: Use technology and innovation to reduce bureaucracy and increase transparency.
- **Tailor Communication**: Adapt messaging to connect with diverse stakeholders, including employees, citizens, and policymakers.
- **Foster Creativity**: Encourage team members to propose innovative solutions to improve services and tackle corruption.

6. Maintaining Focus Amid Corruption

Jesus' Principle

Despite opposition and distractions, Jesus remained focused on His mission. He refused to compromise His values or be drawn into unnecessary disputes (Mark 3:20-30).

Application to Government Leadership

In a corrupt system, maintaining focus requires vigilance, accountability, and resilience. Leaders must create structures that protect their mission from being undermined.

Action Steps

- **Set Guardrails**: Implement checks and balances, such as internal audits and whistleblower protection policies.
- **Cultivate Accountability**: Regularly evaluate programs and policies to ensure alignment with the mission.
- **Resist Compromise**: Stand firm against pressure to conform to corrupt practices, even if it leads to personal sacrifice.

7. Community Engagement With Compassion

Jesus' Principle

Jesus consistently engaged with marginalized individuals and addressed their needs, such as feeding the hungry and healing the sick (Mark 6:34-44, Mark 5:25-34).

Application to Government Leadership

Leaders must prioritize community engagement, focusing on initiatives that address real needs and improve quality of life for all citizens, particularly the underserved.

Action Steps

- **Listen to the Community**: Conduct public forums or surveys to understand citizens' needs and priorities.
- **Implement Practical Solutions**: Focus on programs that deliver measurable benefits, such as housing, healthcare, or education improvements.
- **Build Trust**: Foster open communication with the public, emphasizing transparency and responsiveness.

8. Leaving A Legacy Of Ethical Governance

Jesus' Principle

Jesus prepared His disciples to continue His mission, ensuring His legacy endured (Mark 16:15-20).

Application to Government Leadership

An ethical leader's legacy is measured by the systems and culture they leave behind. By mentoring future leaders and establishing sustainable practices, they ensure their mission continues.

Action Steps

- **Develop Future Leaders**: Mentor and train ethical leaders within the agency to carry forward the mission.
- **Institutionalize Integrity**: Create policies and frameworks that prioritize transparency and accountability.
- **Document Best Practices**: Leave behind a record of successful programs and reforms for future leaders to build upon.

Conclusion

Leading a government agency in a corrupt system is one of the most challenging leadership roles, requiring unwavering integrity, resilience, and faith. By applying Jesus' principles from the Gospel of Mark, a leader can create meaningful change, inspire trust, and improve the quality of life for the communities they serve.

This approach demands a clear mission, ethical leadership, and a commitment to empowering others. With courage, wisdom, and reliance on God, such a leader can navigate systemic obstacles and leave a legacy of transparency, accountability, and service. This kind of leadership not only transforms the agency but also uplifts the community, setting a standard for others to follow.

CASE STUDY: APPLYING JESUS' LEADERSHIP PRINCIPLES TO RAISING A FAMILY IN THE FEAR OF GOD

◆ ◆ ◆

Raising a family in the fear of God and fostering spiritual maturity without reliance on external interference requires intentional leadership, clear values, and steadfast commitment. This approach demands wisdom, resilience, and a focus on building a family culture rooted in the knowledge and application of the scriptures. The leadership principles modeled by Jesus in the Gospel of Mark provide a powerful framework for navigating the complexities of family life, fostering spiritual growth, and addressing challenges with grace.

1. Clarifying The Family's Mission And Vision

Jesus' Principle

Jesus consistently articulated His mission, focusing on proclaiming the Kingdom of God (Mark 1:15). His clarity guided His decisions and inspired those around Him.

Application to Family Life

The family leader must define a clear mission for their household, centering on raising children to know and follow God's Word. This mission becomes the foundation for decision-making, priorities, and daily interactions.

Action Steps:

- **Define a Family Mission Statement**: For example, "To glorify God by growing in faith, love, and obedience to His Word as a family."
- **Communicate the Vision**: Regularly remind family members of the mission through family devotions, discussions, and prayer.
- **Align Activities with the Mission**: Evaluate decisions—such as extracurricular activities, media consumption, and family traditions—based on whether they support spiritual growth.

2. Leading By Example

Jesus' Principle

Jesus modeled the behaviors and values He wanted His disciples to adopt. He led by example in humility, service, and obedience to God's will (Mark 10:45).

Application to Family Life

Children learn more from what they see than from what they are told. The parent must embody the values they want their children to emulate, such as faithfulness, integrity, and humility.

Action Steps:

- **Live Out Biblical Principles**: Show love, patience, and forgiveness in daily interactions.
- **Prioritize Personal Devotion**: Spend time in prayer and Bible study, demonstrating the importance of a relationship with God.
- **Serve the Family**: Engage in acts of service, such as helping with chores or resolving conflicts lovingly, to model Christlike behavior.

3. Teaching Scripture With Depth And Relevance

Jesus' Principle

Jesus used parables and direct teaching to convey spiritual truths in ways that resonated with His audience (Mark 4:1-20). He prioritized clarity and application.

Application to Family Life

Parents are the primary spiritual teachers in the home. Teaching scripture should be intentional, interactive, and tied to real-life application.

Action Steps:

- **Establish Regular Family Devotions**: Set aside time each day or week to read and discuss scripture as a family.
- **Use Real-Life Examples**: Relate biblical lessons to current events, family experiences, or challenges children face.
- **Encourage Questions**: Create a safe space for children

to ask questions about faith and scripture, fostering deeper understanding.

4. Fostering A Culture Of Prayer And Worship

Jesus' Principle

Jesus consistently modeled the importance of prayer, often retreating to solitary places to pray (Mark 1:35). His life was an example of worshipful dependence on God.

Application to Family Life

Prayer and worship should be central to family life, reinforcing dependence on God and gratitude for His provision.

Action Steps:

- **Pray Together Daily**: Begin and end the day with family prayer, including thanksgiving, confession, and intercession.
- **Incorporate Worship into Daily Life**: Sing hymns or worship songs during family time or while doing chores.
- **Teach Individual Prayer**: Encourage each family member to develop their own prayer life.

5. Building Resilience In The Face Of Challenges

Jesus' Principle

Jesus faced opposition and challenges with composure and trust in God's plan. He remained steadfast, using difficulties as opportunities for growth (Mark 4:35-41).

Application to Family Life

Challenges, whether financial, relational, or spiritual, should be addressed with faith and perseverance. The family leader must guide the household in trusting God through trials.

Action Steps:

- **Address Conflicts Biblically**: Resolve disagreements within the family through honest communication and biblical principles like forgiveness and reconciliation.
- **Reinforce Faith in Trials**: Use challenges as opportunities to teach reliance on God and His promises.
- **Celebrate Overcoming Challenges**: Acknowledge and thank God for victories, big or small, as a family.

6. Encouraging Individual Growth

Jesus' Principle

Jesus invested in His disciples' personal growth, giving them responsibilities and equipping them for leadership (Mark 6:7-13).

Application to Family Life

Parents should nurture each family member's spiritual growth, recognizing and developing their unique gifts and abilities.

Action Steps:

- **Assign Age-Appropriate Responsibilities**: Give children tasks that teach responsibility and build confidence, such as leading prayer or organizing family activities.
- **Encourage Scripture Memorization**: Challenge family members to memorize verses that resonate with their personal struggles or goals.
- **Provide Opportunities for Service**: Involve the family in serving others, such as volunteering at church or helping a neighbor.

7. Protecting The Family From External

Interference

Jesus' Principle

Jesus maintained focus on His mission despite opposition and distractions. He managed relationships and situations with wisdom and intentionality (Mark 3:21-35).

Application to Family Life

While engaging with others, the family leader must set boundaries to protect the household from unhealthy influences or unnecessary interference.

Action Steps:

- **Set Clear Boundaries**: Limit external influences, such as media or relationships, that conflict with biblical values.
- **Resolve Disputes Internally**: Avoid involving third parties in family conflicts, focusing on biblical reconciliation instead.
- **Cultivate Discernment**: Teach family members to evaluate external advice or cultural trends through the lens of scripture.

8. Leaving A Legacy Of Faith

Jesus' Principle

Jesus prepared His disciples to continue His mission, ensuring His legacy endured (Mark 16:15-20).

Application to Family Life

The goal of raising a family in the fear of God is to leave a lasting legacy of faith, equipping children to live as mature believers and pass on their faith to future generations.

Action Steps:

- **Document Family Values**: Create a written or verbal record of the family's mission, values, and testimonies to pass down.
- **Celebrate Spiritual Milestones**: Acknowledge baptisms, scripture memorization, or other faith milestones as a family.
- **Encourage Generational Discipleship**: Teach children to disciple others, including future spouses, children, and peers.

Conclusion

By applying Jesus' leadership principles, a parent can create a home that fosters spiritual growth, resilience, and unity. Raising a family in the fear of God requires intentionality, daily reliance on scripture, and a commitment to modeling Christlike behavior. Through prayer, teaching, and nurturing relationships, the family leader can leave a lasting legacy of faith that endures for generations, glorifying God in every aspect of life.

CASE STUDY: APPLYING JESUS' LEADERSHIP PRINCIPLES TO A GROWING CHURCH

◆ ◆ ◆

Imagine a growing church, GracePath Fellowship, with a mission to focus on teaching, worship, and community outreach. This church is committed to developing individuals into maturity in the knowledge and application of the scriptures. Unlike traditional approaches, GracePath avoids reliance on fundraising tactics, extravagant music shows, or the ownership of church property. Instead, it prioritizes simplicity, spiritual depth, and transformative engagement with its community.

The leadership principles modeled by Jesus in the Gospel of Mark provide a framework for guiding GracePath Fellowship as it grows. These principles can help the church maintain its mission, engage effectively with its members and community, and foster sustainable growth.

1. Clarifying Mission And Vision

Jesus' Principle

Jesus had a clear mission: proclaim the Kingdom of God (Mark 1:15). His clarity allowed Him to stay focused despite distractions and opposition.

Application for GracePath Fellowship

The church must articulate a clear and compelling mission: to develop individuals into mature disciples of Christ through teaching, worship, and service. This vision should guide all decisions and activities.

Action Steps:

- **Define a Mission Statement**: "Transforming lives through the teaching of God's Word, authentic worship, and service to our community."
- **Communicate the Vision**: Regularly share the mission with members through sermons, small groups, and church materials.
- **Evaluate Activities**: Ensure every program aligns with the mission of discipleship and community impact.

2. Building And Empowering A Team

Jesus' Principle

Jesus selected a small, diverse group of disciples and invested deeply in their development (Mark 3:13-19). He empowered them to carry forward His mission (Mark 6:7-13).

Application for GracePath Fellowship

Building a team of leaders and volunteers who embody the church's mission is critical. This team should be equipped to lead teaching, worship, and outreach efforts while modeling Christlike maturity.

Action Steps:

- **Recruit Passionate Leaders**: Focus on character, spiritual maturity, and alignment with the church's mission over formal credentials.
- **Train and Equip**: Provide discipleship training and leadership development programs for team members.
- **Delegate Responsibility**: Empower leaders to lead small groups, organize outreach programs, and mentor others in the church.

3. Teaching And Worship With Depth

Jesus' Principle

Jesus taught with authority and simplicity, using parables to connect spiritual truths to everyday life (Mark 4:1-20). His teachings emphasized transformation, not mere knowledge.

Application for GracePath Fellowship

GracePath can emphasize teaching that connects scripture to real-life application, fostering spiritual maturity. Worship services should focus on authenticity and reverence rather than spectacle.

Action Steps:

- **Prioritize Scriptural Depth**: Teach scripture verse by verse, helping members understand context and application.
- **Simplify Worship**: Focus on heartfelt, congregational singing and prayer rather than elaborate productions.
- **Encourage Participation**: Involve members in teaching,

testimony-sharing, and small group discussions to deepen engagement.

4. Community Outreach With Compassion

Jesus' Principle

Jesus consistently met the needs of the people He served. He healed the sick, fed the hungry, and engaged with marginalized individuals (Mark 6:34-44, Mark 5:25-34).

Application for GracePath Fellowship

The church can prioritize outreach that addresses real needs in the community, building relationships and demonstrating God's love.

Action Steps:

- **Identify Community Needs**: Conduct surveys or partner with local organizations to identify pressing needs such as food insecurity or mentorship for youth.
- **Launch Outreach Programs**: Organize simple, impactful initiatives like food distribution, free tutoring, or community cleanup projects.
- **Encourage Member Involvement**: Mobilize the congregation to volunteer in outreach efforts, fostering a culture of service.

5. Avoiding Reliance On Fundraising And Extravagance

Jesus' Principle

Jesus relied on simplicity and trust in God's provision. He sent His disciples out with minimal resources, teaching them to depend on God (Mark 6:8-9).

Application for GracePath Fellowship

GracePath can focus on sustainable, low-cost practices that emphasize stewardship and faith over fundraising campaigns or property ownership.

Action Steps:

- **Leverage Shared Spaces**: Rent community centers, schools, or other facilities for services, avoiding the financial burden of property ownership.
- **Foster Generosity**: Teach members about biblical stewardship and trust God to provide through regular tithes and offerings.
- **Minimize Overhead**: Focus resources on ministry and outreach rather than administrative costs or unnecessary programs.

6. Fostering Growth Through Discipleship

Jesus' Principle

Jesus prioritized making disciples who would carry on His mission. He spent significant time mentoring His disciples, preparing them for leadership (Mark 4:10-12, Mark 6:7-13).

Application for GracePath Fellowship

The church should prioritize one-on-one discipleship and small groups to foster spiritual growth and leadership development.

Action Steps:

- **Small Group Ministries**: Establish home-based small groups for Bible study, prayer, and accountability.
- **Mentorship Programs**: Pair mature believers with newer members for intentional discipleship.
- **Track Spiritual Growth**: Regularly evaluate the spiritual health of members and provide resources for deeper

growth.

7. Navigating Opposition And Challenges

Jesus' Principle

Jesus faced opposition from religious leaders and skeptics but responded with grace, wisdom, and focus on His mission (Mark 2:6-7, Mark 12:13-17).

Application for GracePath Fellowship

As the church grows, it may face criticism for its unconventional approach. Leaders must remain steadfast in their mission, addressing opposition with clarity and grace.

Action Steps:

- **Communicate the Mission**: Reiterate the church's focus on teaching, worship, and outreach when challenged.
- **Engage Critics Constructively**: Respond to criticism with humility and a willingness to listen, while staying true to core values.
- **Strengthen Unity**: Foster a sense of shared purpose among members to withstand external pressures.

8. Leaving A Legacy Of Faith

Jesus' Principle

Jesus prepared His disciples to carry on His mission after His departure, ensuring His legacy continued (Mark 16:15-20).

Application for GracePath Fellowship

The church should focus on creating systems and leaders that sustain its mission for future generations.

Action Steps:

- **Develop Leaders**: Equip members to lead ministries and plant new churches.
- **Document Practices**: Create a "playbook" for church practices and values to guide future leaders.
- **Focus on Succession**: Mentor the next generation of leaders to ensure continuity in vision and mission.

Conclusion

By applying the leadership principles of Jesus, GracePath Fellowship can grow into a thriving church that focuses on spiritual maturity, authentic worship, and meaningful community outreach. These principles provide a roadmap for building a ministry that is faithful to God's Word, impactful in the community, and sustainable over time. By prioritizing simplicity, discipleship, and service, GracePath Fellowship can model a new way of being the church, inspiring others to follow Christ and advance His Kingdom.

APPLICATION IN DIVERSE INDUSTRIES AND LEADERSHIP SETTINGS

◆ ◆ ◆

I have included examples from diverse industries and leadership settings as examples to allows readers to see how Jesus' leadership principles can be applied universally.

---

1. Clarifying Mission and Vision

Industry Example: Healthcare

A hospital's mission, "To provide compassionate, patient-centered care," serves as the foundation for all decision-making. A hospital administrator who aligns resource allocation, staff training, and patient care initiatives with this mission reflects Jesus' focus on clarity of purpose in Mark 1:15.

Modern Insight: Like Jesus' commitment to proclaiming the

Kingdom of God, organizations thrive when leaders ensure every activity supports the core mission, fostering consistency and trust.

2. Leading by Example

Industry Example: Manufacturing

A plant manager facing low morale begins working side-by-side with employees on the production line, demonstrating commitment to their challenges. By modeling diligence and humility, the manager inspires a renewed sense of teamwork, similar to Jesus washing His disciples' feet (John 13:14-15).

Modern Insight: Jesus' servant leadership in Mark 10:45 teaches that leaders inspire by serving and empathizing with their teams.

3. Building and Empowering a Team

Industry Example: Technology Startups

A tech founder delegates key responsibilities to team leads, trusting them to manage engineering, marketing, and product development. By equipping them with resources and authority, the founder mirrors Jesus sending out the twelve disciples in Mark 6:7-13.

Modern Insight: Empowering others through delegation fosters growth, builds confidence, and ensures sustainable leadership.

4. Handling Opposition and Conflict

Industry Example: Politics

A local government official implementing an anti-corruption initiative faces resistance from entrenched interests. By responding with transparency and focusing on ethical principles, the official diffuses opposition and builds public trust, akin to Jesus' calm response to the Pharisees' traps in Mark 12:13-17.

Modern Insight: Jesus' ability to navigate opposition with wisdom shows leaders the value of strategic, mission-focused responses to conflict.

---

5. Innovation and Adaptability

Industry Example: Retail

A retailer struggling to compete with e-commerce platforms adapts by creating a hybrid business model, offering both physical experiences and online convenience. This innovative approach parallels Jesus' use of parables in Mark 4:1-20 to make spiritual truths accessible to diverse audiences.

Modern Insight: Innovation rooted in understanding and responding to stakeholder needs transforms challenges into opportunities.

---

6. Faith as the Foundation of Leadership

Industry Example: Nonprofits

A nonprofit director facing funding shortages trusts

the mission's importance and continues advocating for marginalized communities. Their faith inspires donors and partners to support the cause, reflecting Jesus' resilience in Mark 4:35-41 when calming the storm despite disciples' fears.

Modern Insight: Faith in the mission fuels perseverance and inspires confidence in uncertain circumstances.

---

7. Redefining Success and Failure

Industry Example: Education

A school principal focusing on holistic student development implements programs for mental health, arts, and physical wellness, despite criticism for diverting resources from standardized test preparation. Like Jesus' crucifixion in Mark 15:33-39, which seemed like failure but fulfilled a greater purpose, the principal's efforts yield long-term benefits for the students' overall well-being.

Modern Insight: Success is not always immediate or visible; true leadership often involves prioritizing meaningful, long-term impact over short-term metrics.

---

8. Sacrificial Leadership

Industry Example: Armed Forces

A military leader takes responsibility for a failed operation, shielding their team from repercussions while learning from the experience to prevent future mistakes. This act reflects Jesus' sacrificial leadership, culminating in His death on the cross in Mark 15:33-39.

Modern Insight: Sacrificial leadership builds trust, fosters team loyalty, and demonstrates accountability, key to enduring influence.

---

9. Navigating Betrayal and Building Resilience

Industry Example: Corporate Leadership

A CEO betrayed by a senior executive overcomes the setback by maintaining focus on the company's mission and rebuilding trust with the team. The experience parallels Jesus' betrayal by Judas in Mark 14:43-50 and His resolve to fulfill His mission despite personal pain.

Modern Insight: Effective leaders respond to betrayal with grace and resilience, prioritizing the mission above personal grievances.

---

10. Succession Planning and Legacy

Industry Example: Family Business

A family business owner transitions leadership to the next generation by mentoring them and instilling company values. This mirrors Jesus' preparation of His disciples in Mark 16:15-20, ensuring the continuation of His mission after His ascension.

Modern Insight: Legacy-building involves intentional mentoring, clear communication of values, and gradual transfer of responsibilities.

---

11. Transformative Leadership Through Community Engagement

Industry Example: Urban Development

A mayor transforms a struggling city by partnering with community groups to improve housing, education, and healthcare. This approach reflects Jesus' compassionate leadership in Mark 6:34, where He feeds the five thousand, addressing both spiritual and practical needs.

Modern Insight: Transformative leadership involves holistic strategies that empower communities and address their diverse needs.

Conclusion

By incorporating these detailed examples across various industries—healthcare, technology, education, nonprofits, and more—the book demonstrates the universal applicability of Jesus' leadership principles. These real-world applications make the lessons tangible, helping readers connect timeless spiritual wisdom with the practical realities of leadership in diverse contexts. Through these examples, leaders can envision how to implement these principles in their unique settings, enriching the book's impact and relevance.

APPENDICES

APPENDIX A: SUMMARY OF LEADERSHIP PRINCIPLES FROM THE GOSPEL OF MARK

◆ ◆ ◆

This appendix provides a concise summary of the key leadership principles discussed throughout the book, categorized by chapter:

Chapter 1: Vision and Mission

- Define a clear and compelling mission that guides all decisions.
- Communicate your vision consistently to inspire and align others.
- Stay focused on long-term goals, even amidst distractions or opposition.

Chapter 2: Recruiting and Empowering a Team

- Identify potential in people based on their character and alignment with the mission.
- Build relationships based on trust and mutual respect.
- Delegate responsibilities with clear instructions and provide ongoing support.

Chapter 3: Servant Leadership

- Lead by serving others, prioritizing their needs over personal gain.
- Model humility, compassion, and integrity in all interactions.
- Empower others through actions that inspire and uplift.

Chapter 4: Time Management and Prioritization

- Balance action with reflection, making time for rest and renewal.
- Focus on high-impact activities that align with your mission.
- Manage interruptions with discernment, addressing those that align with your goals.

Chapter 5: Communication Skills

- Use storytelling to connect emotionally and simplify complex ideas.
- Adapt your communication style to suit diverse audiences.
- Listen actively and address opposition with grace and clarity.

Chapter 6: Handling Opposition and Conflict

- Stay composed under pressure and address challenges with wisdom.
- Choose your battles wisely, focusing on issues that advance the mission.
- Turn conflicts into opportunities for growth and alignment.

Chapter 7: Delegation and Trust

- Delegate authority, not just tasks, to empower your team.
- Build trust by supporting team members and embracing their growth.
- Use failures as opportunities for learning and improvement.

Chapter 8: Innovation and Adaptability

- Challenge the status quo thoughtfully, respecting tradition while driving change.
- Adapt to evolving circumstances without compromising core values.
- Foster a culture of creativity and innovation within your team.

Chapter 9: Crisis Management

- Maintain composure during crises to inspire confidence in your team.
- Act decisively while balancing immediate needs with long-term goals.
- Use crises as opportunities to strengthen systems and relationships.

Chapter 10: Legacy and Succession Planning

- Build a legacy by empowering others and communicating a clear vision.
- Develop future leaders through mentorship and gradual transitions.
- Establish sustainable systems to ensure continuity and growth.

APPENDIX B: QUESTIONS FOR REFLECTION AND DISCUSSION

◆ ◆ ◆

These questions can be used for personal reflection or group discussion to deepen understanding of the leadership principles explored in the book.

Personal Reflection

1. What is your personal mission as a leader, and how does it guide your decisions?
2. How do you currently empower others, and where could you improve?
3. How do you handle opposition or criticism, and what can you learn from Jesus' approach?
4. In what ways do you model servant leadership in your organization?
5. What steps have you taken to ensure the continuity of your mission after your tenure?

Group Discussion

1. How can our team better align with our organization's mission and vision?
2. What are some practical ways we can improve delegation and trust within our organization?
3. How do we foster a culture of creativity and adaptability in the face of change?
4. How do we prepare for and manage crises effectively as a team?
5. What is our plan for developing future leaders and ensuring a sustainable legacy?

APPENDIX C: REFERENCES AND FURTHER READING

◆ ◆ ◆

Biblical References

- Gospel of Mark (NIV, ESV, or preferred translation): Primary source for the leadership principles discussed.

Books on Leadership

- *The Servant: A Simple Story About the True Essence of Leadership* by James C. Hunter
- *Leaders Eat Last: Why Some Teams Pull Together and Others Don't* by Simon Sinek
- *The Five Dysfunctions of a Team: A Leadership Fable* by Patrick Lencioni

Articles and Resources

- Harvard Business Review articles on servant leadership, crisis management, and innovation.
- Case studies on mission-driven leadership in business and nonprofit organizations.

APPENDIX D: ABOUT THE AUTHOR

◆ ◆ ◆

Temitope Ajagbe is a seasoned technology executive and leadership expert with over two decades of experience in fostering innovation, building high-performing teams, and navigating complex organizational challenges. His career spans diverse industries, including banking, financial services, technology, and mobile gaming, where he has consistently demonstrated a commitment to excellence, ethical leadership, and transformative impact.

As the Director of Platform Engineering at TruPlay Games, Temitope leads globally distributed teams, develops technology roadmaps, and establishes best practices for security and scalability. His ability to align technical innovation with organizational goals reflects his deep understanding of strategic leadership. Previously, he held key roles at global technology companies like Facebook/Meta, Google, and Amazon, where he implemented solutions that enhanced operational efficiency and fostered growth.

Temitope's academic achievements include a Bachelors in Computer Science from The Universit of Lagos, Nigeria, Master of Science in Computer Science from the University of Texas at San Antonio and ongoing doctoral studies in Management Information Systems. His educational pursuits underscore a lifelong dedication to bridging the gap between technology and leadership.

Temitope's connection to the themes of this book is rooted in his passion for mentorship, team building, and creating systems that empower others. As a Sunday School instructor and community servant, he integrates spiritual principles with practical leadership strategies, inspiring individuals to grow in faith and maturity.

Drawing on his extensive experience in leadership and technology, Temitope brings unique insights into the principles of servant leadership, innovation, and legacy-building. His approach is deeply informed by his faith and commitment to fostering transformative growth in both professional and personal contexts.